DAVIDJI

Davidji

A Collection of Memories

Devotees and Friends Remember
Yogacharya David Hickenbottom

For permission requests, contact the publisher at:
www.crossandlotus.com/contact.html

ISBN: 978-1-957811-09-3 (softcover)
ISBN: 978-1-957811-10-9 (eBook)

All photos courtesy of Carla Hickenbottom Portfolio

Front Cover Photo: David in a riverboat on the Ganges,
Varanasi, India, 2005
Back Cover Photo: David at First Union African Baptist Church,
Daufuskie Island, South Carolina, 2017

Edited by Janice Stevenson

Book design by Jan Westendorp/katodesignandphoto.ca
Cover design based on an original design by Rob Landeros

Published by
The Cross and The Lotus Publishing
Camano Island, Washington, USA

www.crossandlotus.com

Printed and bound in the USA

Davidji

A Collection Of Memories

CONTRIBUTORS

Zachary Abbey, Susan Bakes,
George Baldigara, Honor Baldigara,
Rebecca Barnowe, Rick Bohr,
Maureen Chlopan, Geri DiCicco,
Dylan Dreiling, Judy Ellis,
Rick Ellis, Charmie Gilcrease,
Shruti Ranga Gowda, Corliss Harmer,
Rebecca Harvey, Carla Hickenbottom,
Lois Hickenbottom, Greg Hough,
Jill Hough, Briana Jones, Catherine Kelley,
Cate Koler, Larry Koler, Ruth Lamb,
Sarah Leonard, Mira Lutz, Rolf
Mayrhofer, Michele Rogan, Peter Schultz,
Adam Shinn, Janice Stevenson,
Dianne Tipton, Jerry Trofimchuk,
Phyllis Victory, and Rose Wylie

CONTENTS

EDITOR'S NOTE:

THOSE WHO KNEW Yogacharya David Hicken-bottom as guru, fellow disciple, and friend were invited to contribute to this book of memories. The result is a variety of styles and voices—some have titles, some do not; some follow American punctuation rules, some follow Canadian rules; some follow strict grammar guidelines, some are freer in expression. Editing was kept to a minimum.

The experiences are presented anonymously, to encourage the sharing of private as well as public moments. They are revealed here in the hope of inspiring, informing, comforting, and sometimes amusing fellow seekers on the path.

"ONE OF THE WONDERFUL things about a guru is that they are human. And we see their humanity, and through that we come to believe that this human, this self of who we are, can achieve some degree of realization. It gives us hope. It gives us a bridge. It gives us a link to the Divine. Otherwise, God always seems somewhere out of our reach, somewhere beyond us. But a true master, a true guru, makes God feel as close and as near and as dear as our best friend, as our next breath, as a thought that flows through us, as the very life that animates this body. This is the quality of a true guru, and through their being we might be uplifted and feel our oneness."

FROM A TALK BY YOGACHARYA DAVID
HICKENBOTTOM ON AUGUST 1, 1999

Foreword

DAVID HICKENBOTTOM WAS my closest and dearest friend in this lifetime. We shared so much of life, both the spiritual and the mundane. We shared a dedication to our guru, Mother Hamilton and the spiritual path. These things were uppermost in our minds and filled our daily lives. Though we did many regular things together, it was rare that we didn't talk about spiritual subjects even during these times.

In the early days of our friendship, we went to movies and walks and restaurants together. Often, we were accompanied by others, but we were very content to just be in each other's company. David lived with me and my children in the late 1970s, renting a room in my three-bedroom student housing apartment. It was during this time that we got to attend some of the same university classes. We were lucky to be able to take classes in Eastern religions and philosophy from Dr. Frank Conlon. Professor Conlon was one of those teachers in our lives that we felt completely at home with because his interests and insights were contagious, well explained, and always thought provoking. So, we signed up for every class of his that fit our schedules. (My wife Cate also took several classes taught by him in the 1980s.)

We had classes together in religious studies and early Christian history. Again, we tended to follow just one professor, Dr. Michael Williams. He introduced us to the new area of study associated with the Nag Hammadi cache of ancient documents. During one semester we got to meet Elaine Pagels when Professor Williams invited her to visit the University of Washington to give a talk. She was deeply immersed in this specific field of study and wrote several books that we were reading at the time.

Finally, I will mention the opportunity that we both had to meet Dr. Ramchandra Gandhi, Mahatma Gandhi's grandson. He spent a whole semester teaching two classes: one, a history class on his grandfather and the other in his own field, which was philosophy. Professor Gandhi was a very sweet and unassuming man. He was very easy to talk to and was very knowledgeable about all things philosophical and religious—and in both Western and Eastern contexts.

Charmell audited the class on the Mahatma and at the end of the semester she invited him

to a dinner that she put on so that he could meet
Mother Hamilton. Of course, David and I both
were invited, too. It was most interesting. Mother
was so natural around him. At the end of the visit,
he asked to speak to Mother privately and they
spent about 10 minutes together in the dining
room while the rest of us sat in the living room.
As I was driving him back, he mentioned that
Mother had helped him with some decision he
was struggling with.

I remember David being quite put out by the
way that Professor Gandhi was treated by other
professors who were sitting in at a few of the
early philosophy class meetings. They were quite
dismissive of some of his ideas. David felt it was
disrespectful and he quit the class early. I think
he was just auditing it anyway. David really hated
injustice and disrespect. I struggled with this
inwardly as I continued in the class. Being dispu-
tative may have been common in this field and
at the graduate level which this class was. It may
have been that the University of Washington had
that sort of reputation. I never got a resolution on
this. Professor Gandhi never complained, nor did
he talk about it.

The examples above were things that informed
our conversations for many years. We learned so
many of these things together and so it bonded

us on the intellectual plane. Because of our focus on our guru, we already had a spiritual and emotional bond. These experiences cemented our relationship. I found in David someone who had a very fine mind, and we developed a collaborative way of thinking about issues. I can't emphasize enough how our university schooling affected us. We may have been fellow students before in other lifetimes. I have sometimes wondered if we were fellow monks or priests, too.

One distinction comes to me as I write this and that is that the Hindu or Eastern teachings were areas that David really excelled in and that my interests or predilections were aimed more toward the Christian teachings. These are due to small differences in our orientations but as I think about it, it seems to be true.

David and I grew up just 50 miles away from each other and during our childhood it's likely that we passed each other while traveling between Sunnyside and Yakima or the Tri-Cities. Perhaps we looked at one another and a thought passed between us. When we did meet in 1976, it was at church service at Bonnie's house in Northeast Seattle. I usually sat toward the front of the room and David often sat at the back, sometimes in the small library just to the rear of the living room.

The library was opened up for overflow when that was required.

There was David in the back, bearded, quiet and calm. He came whenever he could get away from his job at his father's business in Sunnyside, Washington. Later, he moved to the Seattle area and we saw more of him and on a more regular basis.

David's early life and working life was centered around business, warehouses, and trucking. He drove the big rigs that his father owned and other vehicles like forklifts and utility trucks. He had many funny stories about that life in Sunnyside. There were employees of his father's business that he knew for many years growing up and these were mostly men and mostly men with character. They were also interesting characters. I wish I could recall those stories with more detail, but I am unable to do so.

He used to enjoy driving forklifts in the warehouse, maneuvering wildly and timing things just right to pick up and deposit the pallets quickly but also for the sheer enjoyment and exhilaration of that speed and ability. The young men that he worked with were conscientious but also fun to compete with and liked to test their competence against each other.

David was very funny himself and he loved humorous jokes, puns, and stories. He often used the term "guy humor" when it was about something he understood well from his western American perspective. Obviously, it wasn't just humor for "guys" but what he was saying was that this joke or humorous story really appealed to people of his background, and these were mostly men—or "guys."

Since David and I grew up in an almost identical cultural milieu he and I clicked easily from the start. Many of Mother's devotees and disciples were comfortable in the culture of Seattle and Washington state in those days. We were of the 1960s post-war generation which was set in the world by God to make changes. We all felt it. But Mother was there—in our case—to show where that energy should be directed. It should be directed to God and Self-realization. David was better than most at following this redirection, this signpost on the road to his destiny, to mankind's destiny of future ages.

Mother always taught us that we were the pioneers in a new spiritual age and that what Master brought to the West was the synthesis of the highest teachings of East and West. Looking back, I see that David took this to heart more than most of us. He truly adored Mother in every respect and in every aspect of herself, both human and divine. If you study his writings and talks you will find that he thoroughly blended Mother's teachings into his own. He was her first-born son.

He now sits at her side in whatever exalted place they share. They are constantly watching everything we do here. They direct us when we need them. May we always be worthy of their love and help.

REV. LAWRENCE KOLER

A True Disciple

I WAS WALKING toward a hug with Mother Hamilton after her talk, back in about 1978, when I looked down at a young man still seated. His eyes were looking up as to a glorious star, full of bliss. That was my first sight of David. I called him Bliss-Out back then. I could see he was a remarkable soul.

om sri ram jai ram jai jai ram om sri ram jai ram jai jai ram

WHEN I THINK ABOUT DAVID it is always in connection with Mother. I met Mother in 1978 at Bonnie's house. Mother was at the top of the stairs glowing! I had met the person I was looking for my whole life. Looking back now it was such a short life at 19, but from the time I was four I was looking for that Light that I saw in Mother.

My relationship with David starts with Mother. I first noticed him when Mother stopped her talk and said something to a person I couldn't see. If memory serves, she had him stand up and was speaking rather harshly to him. I wondered who he was and why he was getting 'yelled' at. I sat very still; I did not want to have her turn her attention to me in that way!

After some time of going to services I had some questions for Mother and she said that she was very busy but that I should talk to David about these questions. I had a very difficult time trusting and Mother recommending David to me put that, and in most ways, him, above reproach. Sometimes I think that she gave David the hard cases like me so that he would get some good practice in!

With Mother, I saw only Light and Beauty, Intelligence and Grace and couldn't imagine that I could become what she was. With David I was able to see the human and I was in a raw state with him. Raw, meaning I was rough around the edges and didn't have the same deference with him that I did with Mother. That changed as time went on.

I didn't know how I should feel in social situations. When someone said something and I laughed, people looked at me funny, or other odd reactions on my part. I remember "planning" how I should react in different scenarios so that it would come across as genuine. The saying is 'fake it until you make it', and I did—both.

Mother showed me the goal and David showed me the path. And kept lovingly guiding me when I fell, or resorted to kicking me in the backside when I needed it! If Mother would have chastised me the way David did, I don't know if I would have been able to handle it, but her relationship with me was all about Love, showing me that I was worthy of that Love. Then when I was beginning to feel worthy, David showed me that every thing I did was not worthy! I was worthy but my actions needed to reflect Who I Am and when they did not, I was guided—either internally or externally.

Once David was quite harsh with me about an action and it devastated me. He called the next day to apologize and let me know that Mother had rebuked him for speaking to me in such a manner. That was a great lesson to see David so humble and contrite—for me! It was quite a needed boost to my self-esteem.

When I was going through some very tough situations David was there, several times a day at one point. Just listening, saying breathe, you have the answers, you will get through this. Taking me to dinner, walks or just sitting at home talking, showing me how to be human. So patient, so caring. For a while I was writing every day and he was responding almost every day. After a bit he let me know that God told him that he could only write to me occasionally. It was a kind way of saying you can walk on your own now.

om sri ram jai ram jai jai ram om sri ram jai ram jai jai ram

A BLESSED PRIVILEGE

I CONSIDER MYSELF very blessed to have had a divine friendship with Yogacharya David, a spiritual brother through our own beloved Mother and Guru, Mother Hamilton.

I have a vague memory of my first glimpse of David, probably in 1976. I don't remember if it was the first time I made the pilgrimage from Victoria to Seattle to visit Mother or the next, but I recall getting up from my chair after Service, beginning to move towards the queued devotees who were lining up to hug Mother, and looking over at a man, still seated, who was obviously in a very deep meditative state. Although I was very new to all of this, I could tell that he was in a deeper meditation than anyone I had seen before, and something about him impressed me enough to not forget him. However, it was not until the fall of 1979 that I actually met David, through Larry.

I have many memories of doing lots of everyday fun things with David and his wife—like going to the movies, out for a meal etc. He and Larry were close friends and they shared many spiritual conversations, but my relationship with David at that time was pretty much just friendship-based. However, I sensed his complete loyalty to Mother and the path and a keen sense of dharma. This intensified as he took on the role of minister for Mother.

During the last years of the 1980s Mother continued to have physical illnesses and more and more devotees were not attending services. I began to know Davidji better as there were fewer and fewer of us in the group. A year or so after Mother's Mahasamadhi, David went into his "dark night of the soul" and took some sabbatical time. Larry and I began to host services in our home. David eventually came out of his dark night and his inner light began to shine brighter. He stayed with us off and on during this time and discussions were ongoing about Mother's teachings and how we would continue her work and mission.

What was most amazing about being David's friend was having a front-row seat to witness the transformation of an "ordinary" man into a God-man. David, when I met him, was a fellow devotee, one of us. Yet, unknown to many of us, although not Larry nor of course, Mother, he was going through intense spiritual experiences, and by 1989 Mother had appointed him to be her successor as she could see not only his spiritual advancement but the potential for great leadership capabilities.

David was Mother's choice as successor. I was there when she made the announcement and I never questioned that. However, I am not proud to say that for a number of years I did not recognize David's rising spiritual attainment. No one could replace Mother in my heart and soul and for me no one could take her place nor reach anywhere near her attainment. Perhaps our friendship, which had always been somewhat casual to this point, was partially to blame and there was an over-familiarity.

One time, when I was perhaps disagreeing with something David said or did, I heard Mother say to me inwardly—but it was like I could hear it out loud, like she had one of those old-fashioned megaphones directly in my ear—"This is my beloved son, in whom I am well pleased." This profoundly affected me, and I realized I had to trust him as the spiritual leader.

By the mid-1990s David began to attract his own devotees, and what wonderful souls they were. Yet I, and likely other devotees of Mother's, held back, unable to allow ourselves to fully join with them and embrace what was pouring out of his soul, no doubt retarding our own advancement at this time. But as David devoted more time to his and Mother's devotees and developed his own way of expressing the Truth he continued to experience, I began to value his wisdom and was impressed with the concern and care he gave all those with whom he interacted. On a number of occasions, I contacted him for spiritual advice, and it was always wise, compassionate, and insightful. You always felt completely safe with David. He was by nature a protector, both physically and spiritually.

Two separate periods in David's sadhana intensely transformed him—his visit to India in 1998/99 and his year of silence at Cloud Mountain. I was privileged to have toured with him part of that time in India and participated in all of his retreats at Cloud Mountain. When David came back into the world after his silence he stayed in our home until his marriage to Carla, and it was wonderful to have him with us, particularly at that time, as the spiritual ambiance which came from him was very powerful.

David modeled for me, and I am sure for many, how to be the perfect sadhaka. He was very one-pointed in his goal. He flew past us all—his was the airplane route—but always so lovingly, he would turn and extend his hand to us, lifting us up so we too could aspire to the same lofty peaks. I was in awe at the speed with which he was scaling the heights and also, I must admit, jealous. Why were my longings for God unrewarded by the Lord? Why were my efforts and sadhana so much more unproductive? I did come to realize that comparison and jealousy should play no part in the devotee's journey to God—one can be inspired by others, but it is for us to step out in faith, with full trust and assurance, that God's grace is with us in full measure.

Mother's mission, like her Master's, was to unite East and West in a common spiritual language. Mother was unique; as she said: "I went the way and therefore can tell you about the way." Mother gave the world a new scripture, one that united the mystical truths of all religions, relating how the historical events of the Bible were inner spiritual experiences. David knew Mother's teachings to be true; he lived them and experienced them. He spent the rest of his life refining those teachings in the many lessons he wrote, the workshops he led, the sermons he gave. He applied them to studies on The Gita, The Ramayana, and the life of Christ. David shared his life as an aspirant in such writings as My Spiritual India, and in his journals from Cloud Mountain we get an intimate glimpse into the heights he is attaining. He masterly developed practical lessons for his students, for sadhakas everywhere, in his Notes to Sadhakas. This is an important part of the legacy he leaves us.

The last several years with David were so special for me. I was privileged to work with him for a number of projects and publications as his editor and he allowed me to have a voice in plans for Mother's work. Larry and I were fortunate to host him and Carla for Service most Sundays when they were not traveling.

Our Davidji had become a great Light. Standing before him after his Sunday talk, with hands posed in pranam, looking into his deep and fathomless eyes and then melting into the love and bliss of his hug, I worshipped my Mother in his arms. No longer Guru and Disciple, they were One, and I the fortunate third in this moment of blessed Trinity.

A few days before Yogacharya David left the body he said words to me I will never forget. They are etched into my soul: "It has been my greatest privilege serving God in you." Humble, loving, and giving, just days before his passing. What a great God-man he was and is. I was so blessed to have known him.

om sri ram jai ram jai jai ram om sri ram jai ram jai jai ram

FINDING DAVID

I FIRST MET DAVID at the very first talk he gave in Vancouver in December 1995. He had just come out of the "Dark Night of the Soul" and Phyllis opened her home to have him there. I recognized the truth in his words and felt the love of God. I "just knew" then that I was committed and it was where I needed to be. After almost 28 years, I still believe that to be true.

Even though there have been some difficult lessons along the way, I have been deeply changed.

om sri ram jai ram jai jai ram om sri ram jai ram jai jai ram

THE FIRST TIME I met David was at his first talk he did in Vancouver! I must admit I did not understand half of what he said or any of the names of people he talked about.

After a time, I started to learn about yogis and Mother Hamilton (not Mother Earth, my first thought). As the years passed on, I got to know David more and more. When we would get together, the talks I had with David were so special for me. He taught me how to deal with anger issues, how to forgive, compassion and how to open a door to let some light in.

David had a special way of guiding me through obstacles rather than telling me what to do.

David was my way to the Light.

Missing him so very much.

om sri ram jai ram jai jai ram om sri ram jai ram jai jai ram

MEETING THE MASTER

OFTENTIMES IN OUR LIVES, we are oblivious to the guiding hand of God. It is only in looking back with hindsight, that we catch a glimpse of the tremendous intelligence guiding all creation. As I look back at the circumstances surrounding my meeting with David, I am overcome by awe and gratitude.

I had been a spiritual aspirant for many years before coming into contact with David. My pursuits had brought me great growth and wonderful spiritual experiences. But due to a tremendously difficult couple of years, I felt like I had stopped making progress. My soul yearned for something more.

It was during a cross-country move from eastern Canada to Oregon that I felt inspired to revisit one of my favorite books, *Autobiography of a Yogi*, in audio form. State by state flew by as I became entranced by the magic of Master's words. I felt a tremendously powerful vibration emanating from every experience during this transformational time, and I felt a deep connection to our lineage of masters.

It was upon arriving at our new home in Ashland, Oregon, that I lay on the veranda in the midday sun. With a deep devotional prayer, I prayed to Babaji to bring me a Guru who he thought was worthy of being called a spiritual master. Immediately, I was enveloped in tremendous bliss. In my ecstasy, an answer to my prayer felt imminent.

The very next day, my mother mentioned that she ran into a wonderful man a couple of houses down by the name of Peter Schultz. Yogananda came up during the conversation and she said that her son (myself) was obsessed with the master and had been reading his book nonstop. We were both invited to church that coming Monday. During that church service, I was introduced to Mother's and David's pictures, and we listened to a wonderful talk by David that I found tremendously inspiring. After service, I thanked Peter and made my way back home, ready for a good night's sleep. Nothing would really prepare me for what would come next.

That night in my dreams, I found myself in a wondrously beautiful garden, filled with roses, gardenias, and trickling fountains. It was situated at the precipice of a hill, overlooking a bay, with mountains beyond the water in the distance. On the property was a lovely little bungalow, overlooking the view. After I admired the setting, I became aware that there was someone with me. To my astonishment, there stood David before me, smiling radiantly in a beautiful white robe. I felt so safe and secure in this place with David, and a childlike innocence began to express itself through me. I ran through the grass and laughed with joy—feeling tremendously free in the ethereal sunlight.

The next morning upon awakening, I was shocked by the dream, but felt so grateful for the experience. From that point, night after night for weeks and months, David returned in my dreams. I began to feel so intimate and familiar with this master whom I had never met in person.

When I was finally able to meet him almost a year later, his opening statement to me was "It's wonderful, to finally meet in the body."

Shortly after I became aware of David, he left the body. I only had the opportunity to meet him once in the physical world. But I feel that he was preparing me to connect with his soul and essence, rather than becoming attached to his physical form.

om sri ram jai ram jai jai ram om sri ram jai ram jai jai ram

ALTHOUGH I KNEW about Mother and having heard talks of hers, I wasn't moved to follow this path. I thought it really wasn't for me. After a few years I met David at a workshop and a couple of years later attended a service held by him. At the same time, I was given a copy of *Autobiography of a Yogi* and these two events completely changed my attitude. I felt like this was the path and I should enter into it. However, upon reflection I felt that with a decision of this magnitude that perhaps I should get an affirmation from God.

A little while later just before waking I heard a voice loud and clear stating "David is always with you". I woke up and again loud and clear "David is always with you". There was my sign. Now even though David is no longer in the body I'm comforted by knowing David is always with me.

om sri ram jai ram jai jai ram om sri ram jai ram jai jai ram

A TOUCHSTONE

DAVID WAS MY TOUCHSTONE, my way of seeing what I could become by watching his actions, his words, listening to his guidance. He was also a touchstone of the old meaning, 'rubbing my actions, thoughts, words by him to see if they were the Gold of Spirit, or common ego thoughts.' He led me, guided me.

After Mother died and David took up duties again around 1995, I wrote to Swamiji and asked him whether it was a good idea for me to trust David. Swamiji said David was a good one.

One Christmas Service at Larry and Cate's, around 1997, I was sitting in the back and there was a Christmas tree to my left and the kitchen doorway to my right. David was at the window facing us. There was a presence to my right and a hand on my shoulder. I turned around and no physical presence was there, but Mother was there. She gestured to David and back to me, and to David again. Without words she was saying that she was 'giving' me to him, and I was to follow him.

om sri ram jai ram jai jai ram om sri ram jai ram jai jai ram

RECENTLY, PETER SCHULTZ asked me how I came to this path; he asked, "Wasn't it pretty much of a miracle?" I said, "Yes it was." His question, plus the fourth anniversary of my first trip to Seattle, prompted me to put the story into written form.

Rather at the last minute I was prompted to volunteer to drive a truck full of bicycles from Indiana to Seattle for a Unity Church based group. Cricket, the woman in charge, kept asking me during the drive out, "Now, who do you know in Seattle?" I told her cheerfully, more than once, "No one." I remember telling her that it was a kind of pilgrimage for me. I had a sense of "adventures ahead" and a feeling of optimism. Once we had arrived I stayed in the basement of the Unity Church with the teens and helped with different group activities. The Unity Group was composed of a large group of teens plus chaperones who would be pedaling from Seattle to Los Angeles. When I had breaks I went up to the Chapel to meditate.

On Saturday, June 20th I went up to the Chapel to meditate and I met Glory. She told me there would be a meditation ceremony taking place soon. I said, "I'll be only a few minutes." I got quiet and asked, should I go to the Bo Diddley concert or should I help in the kitchen down-stairs? God said, "STAY RIGHT HERE." There was no mistaking that message: I knew that I was being directed to go to the meditation ceremony and I felt a thrill of peaceful excitement. So, I went downstairs to change into clean clothes. While I was downstairs, Jill approached me to ask about where the children would stay and I helped negotiate with the Unity group so that a partitioned area was created and toys were located for the children of those attending the meditation ceremony.

As I came back up the stairs, I saw a lot of people with flowers and fruit and some of them were very dressed up. At this point I did get a little nervous because I realized that this was a very big event that people had prepared for. Jill recognized me (she said I looked kind of lost) and asked me if she could help and I just said, "I'm supposed to be here." She said, "You need to talk to David."

Jill then went in the Chapel and brought David out to talk to me. David asked me if I could come to a service tomorrow in West Seattle. I said, "Yes." Then he named the Gurus and asked me if I accepted this lineage. With the same clarity I had when God told me "STAY RIGHT HERE" I knew intuitively to say "YES." It was so nice that the others gave me flowers and fruit to offer since I didn't have any. I remember that someone shared a gerbera daisy that was particularly lovely. As I looked around the chapel, many faces looked familiar even though I had never met them before. During the beginning of the ceremony, my ego said, "You can leave anytime if you don't agree with anything." But there was nothing to object to and so the ego fell into the background as I soaked in the lovely spiritual energy that permeated everything.

All through the Kriya Service and Initiation I felt a deep sense of being home. This is the spiritual path I had been searching for, for such a long time. I knew that this was the whole reason for my coming to Seattle, for coming such a long way. I especially remember the Aums and the Rose Song: how they soothed my soul to the core. I felt like a person who had been lost in the desert who finally gets to drink.

The next day (Sunday) Charmie and Mike picked me up to go to the service at Cate and Larry's in West Seattle. In the car I thought: for spiritual people, they sure drive like devils! When I saw the big picture of Mother, I couldn't take my eyes off of her. I felt Mother and Master's presence very strongly. After the service, we went to Mother's gravesite where I felt more wonderful spiritual energy. On my plane ride back they asked for volunteers to take a later flight from

Midway to Indianapolis in exchange for a free ticket. I was up in a flash and I knew that this free ticket was for going back to Seattle to find a job. I already knew that I would be moving there and that God was giving me the ticket.

om sri ram jai ram jai jai ram om sri ram jai ram jai jai ram

MANY YEARS AFTER her Mahasamadhi in 1991, my beautiful Satguru, Mother Hamilton, surprised me with a very special gift. This Divine blessing came in 2010 when she inwardly prompted me to attend one of the retreats held twice a year by her ordained successor, the Reverend Yogacharya David Hickenbottom. This first satsang with Davidji proved to be the beginning of an indescribably wonder-filled nine years of "Ram-adventures" and "God-walks" with him, the likes of which fill me with memories that will forever remain deeply embedded in my heart. What follows are a couple of them . . .

Upon learning that devotees were gathering together in silent, six-hour meditations once a month with Davidji, I knew I had to join them! After all, this would provide me with another invaluable opportunity to be in his Divine Presence again, something I'd now begun desiring more and more. I sure hadn't disciplined my body, though, to sit still for that long period of time, so when Davidji asked me how I had made out after that first attempt, I admitted that my back had really given me a hard time.

The following month I sat again with Davidji and the others for this extended meditation, and once more was asked by my caring Teacher, as I stood by the door to leave, how I had faired this time. I responded by saying something to the effect that I hadn't felt any back pain at all that time. Instead, though, I told him that I'd been bothered by a very unusual new pain, and that it had taken precedence over the other one! David then said that he and his beloved Carla would pray for me. When he uttered those words, spoken so quietly and unassumingly, I remember instantly feeling something. In all the years that passed, I never could put my finger on what this "something" was, up until this very morning, that is, when the answer came: "What you felt was the **power** behind Master David's words, and that his words carried weight!"

A couple of days later, in a doctor's office, I heard this compassionate caregiver say to me: "Oh, you poor thing, you have shingles." I was given something to take for this viral infection, but was also cautioned that the medication might not work because I possibly had waited too long to have this problem checked out. Well, within about week I was healthy again. The shingles were completely gone!

om sri ram jai ram jai jai ram om sri ram jai ram jai jai ram

FIRST MEETING WITH DAVID

IN THE MID 90's I began visiting with Lois at swim meets (our boys swam together). The talk turned to spiritual talk quickly. We found we had a lot in common. Lois invited me to come to meditation at her house on Wednesday nights. It wasn't long before David was coming for a visit and talk. Of course, by this time, I knew quite a bit about David and was excited to meet him and hear him talk.

There were questions and discussion at the end. I remember telling David that I had a lot of spiritual ideals I could talk about and freely did. I'd watched others a lot, but learned from them, rather than find out for myself. To this David replied, "Well . . . are you ready to start living it for yourself?" Me, "Yes!" David, "Well then, let's get on with it." And, boy, that's exactly what happened. Since that time, I do not have spiritual discussions with people much. God has silenced me in that realm, but I am living it for myself.

Moving forward, the idea became clear in a recent class I participated in: we are called by our guru to attend Kriya initiation and that guru gets us there. Kriya initiation was set in June (1998?). I was not planning on attending due to a work commitment that there was no way I could get out of. Plans had been made and confirmed. A week before Kriya was to be held, I read Chapter 26 in *Autobiography of a Yogi*, "The Science of Kriya Yoga," and knew I had to attend Kriya initiation. Within two days everything changed and I was on my way to Kriya initiation with Lois and Chad. I did not do a thing; it was all done for me.

om sri ram jai ram jai jai ram om sri ram jai ram jai jai ram

I MET DAVID at Al and Elaine's in Vancouver which was a turning point in my life. I cannot say it turned that evening; however, it planted a seed, and I felt I was getting closer to the truth.

My life at that time was full of questions and chaos. David inspired a direction and a truth so I could drop the chaos. This took time and much guidance and support from David which he gave so lovingly and willingly. He showed how God could mend my broken heart and give me hope. My life changed after meeting David and I am ever so grateful. Many memories of David at Christmas and I loved the New Year's Eve meditations.

om sri ram jai ram jai jai ram om sri ram jai ram jai jai ram

FROM THE TIME I first heard about Yogacharya David, around the summer of 2014, he had an extraordinary impact on my life. And yet, it took more than a few years before a first personal encounter occurred between us. That was because as much as I felt drawn to him, as often as I listened to his and Mother's talks with rapt attention and awe, and as often as I perceived the tremendous depth of his mere presence on Camano Island, I nonetheless needed to know that he was in my life by God's Will alone, and not from any personal desire of my own, to jump from one teacher to the next.

I was already a disciple of Yogananda. I was already on a path of 'self-realization,' and filled to the brim with the outflowing-inspiration to create a yoga-farm community. So, despite the incredible sense of wonder that David had already awakened in me, I waited. And I waited. To see if God would reveal Himself to me, in David.

That is, until one night in a satsang-style gathering, a comment was made to the group, that this life is for preparing for the next one. That, "perhaps in the next life, we can sit at the feet of our Guru."

The expressed sentiment had a shocking effect on my nature. I inwardly revolted. I went home that night to my meditation closet. I cried tears of anguish to God and to Master. This cannot be my truth. This is not my truth. For many nights, I do not know how many, I pleaded to God to introduce me to my Guru in this life. The thought of not knowing my Guru, here and now, was enough to destroy all peace of mind, and any sense of contentment for any kind of 'progress' I had made up until this point. I felt as if I had done nothing, and that I could not rest until God helped me.

Within some number of days or weeks (I do not know how many), with this prayer silently, relentlessly repeating in my heart and mind, a miraculous thing happened. As I was 'manning' the farm booth at the Camano Farmers Market, I looked up to see David in the flesh, standing about 10 feet from the farm table, outside the stand. Immediately I recognized him. He was with Carla, also, who I recognized because of her frequent visits to the market, though I didn't realize who she was.

Nerves got the best of me for one frozen moment, but I seized the next one. I jumped out from the booth and approached him, now towards the middle of the courtyard-style market. "Are you Yogacharya David?" "I am," he beamed with so much natural joy. I took the opportunity to 'spill the beans'; to tell him how much inspiration he had shared with me over the last many years. He was gracious, joyful and kind.

I have since been told that he jokingly referred to himself as 'famous,' after my having gawked and been in awe at that introduction. Indeed, he was already the most famous person in my heart of hearts. For me, it was the encounter I had waited for, in so many days, months, years. The one, whereby God brought his Son to meet me.

Following that brief, yet blessed introduction, I recall that he published a blog later that week about being "Touched by Saints." It seems also, that he spoke in his talk that week, about "Saints in your backyard." Though of course he made no mention of his own saintliness in either his writing or talk, I yet found myself basking in the sun of being 'touched' by a Saint. For I had just met one at the farmers market.

It didn't take long for a second conversation, which happened soon after, when I answered the farmhouse phone and found David on the other end. He called and signed up for the next farm supper, which at that time we hosted once a month during the growing season. He made a reservation for four: himself, Carla, Larry and Cate.

In the buildup to his coming, I was equal parts anxious and delighted. Since our encounter at the market, I had continued to spend many mornings and evenings in his presence, in the silence of my inner life.

When he arrived at the farm, amidst forty or so other guests, I spotted him when he ascended the verandah porch, directly above the yard where the dinner was to be hosted. I walked up from the yard, like a bee to flower. He saw me and gifted me with the most wonderful and unexpected hug that I have ever received. He embraced me with such simple-knowing and a most beautiful, genuine smile. Like an old Friend, not someone I had just met.

It was around this time as well, that one of our ashram-mates had approached me, and said ardently, "You need to sit with the people tonight! You can't be serving with us; you should be at a table with the guests." In the handful of years of hosting these suppers, it had never occurred to me that I could sit at a table. The mere act of hosting a farm dinner was the kind of 'all hands on deck' situation that demanded the willingness to do whatever was necessary, at any moment. But this afternoon was indeed different. David and the party of four sat at a six-person table in the middle of the farmyard. My partner at that time and I happily sat down with them, directly across the circle-table from David.

It was here that David began to talk to me directly, and to share with us all. I vividly remember his describing Mother's few policies regarding her ministry: not to advertise; not to charge money for the services rendered; and not to have an organization.

Oh my God. It was like music for my Soul, and a few tears of joy ran down my face as he spoke. Here was I, placed in an organization by beloved Master, serving and accepting all its ways as best as I could, yet always knowing that it wasn't the way of my Self. When David spoke these words, the knowing of their truth, as my own, was direct from the Source, speaking to my need for clarity in that very moment. These of course weren't to be my own literal rules for operating the farm; but rather, to live them in spirit, inside of myself.

He also told us of his first meeting with Mother Hamilton: the feeling that she imparted in him, the experiences in the aftermath of that meeting, and the gradual realization of the impact she began having on his consciousness.

He spoke of a time at dinner with Mother and the group, I believe at a restaurant. Mother specifically began talking to him, though the others were all still present. In this moment, he felt her envelope him in a bubble, whereby no one else could hear them. As he recounted this story, I became suddenly aware of the bubble in which I had now become ensconced. Though there were many other farm residents serving, and a few dozen guests all around us, it was as though nobody outside of the table was able to perceive the stature of the One who now sat in the backyard amongst us. The impact of my own knowing brought more tears, and especially as he looked across the table at me.

Eventually, the time came in the evening when I was to rally the entire dinner's attendees, take them on a farm tour through the different gardens, and to visit the various farm animals. These walking tours are especially when I aspire to share the Yoga-Farm philosophy that we have embraced, of simplicity, Nature, and Love, as the guiding forces of our community life. This meant that I would now be walking David (and all the guests of the evening) around the farm and doing a lot of the talking. The absolute last thing I would have chosen to do, would be to have to talk in front of Him! I only wanted to listen, and receive, and listen some more. But I also knew, this was indeed my part to play in this scene of the movie, and I simply had to do that which was mine to do. It was only a few minutes into my introductory sharing that I was able to relax some. For there was not a shred of judgment or critique from David; rather, only kindness and loving support emanated from him.

At the end of the tour, some 45 minutes of walking and talking about the farm, an extra special blessing took place. As we finished the loop and walked in the general direction of the dinner-grounds, I found that suddenly David and I were alone. This had never in my recollection happened: that I walked with only one person to end the tour. Rather, there would typically be a dozen or two with me in our return for the dessert portion of the dinner. Yet, here was just David and myself, and we walked side by side. He took my arm and interlocked it with his own. I don't remember saying a word, nor whether he said anything either. I was in step with my Guru, and in his loving arms. We walked arm in arm to the farm store, where I had the darshan to gift him a comfrey oil which we make on the farm; and he, in turn, bought a comfrey oil for Reverend Larry, whose birthday it was that day.

And surely, it was mine as well. Born anew in the family of Mother and David.

om sri ram jai ram jai jai ram om sri ram jai ram jai jai ram

HOW MY LIFE CHANGED after meeting David, so so
so much!!!

It changed before I met him. A friend requested
for me to pray for her spiritual teacher, and while
I was praying for him, I began to feel very connected. My life changed in many subtle ways.

Then I finally decided to meet David. It was
at a service in Seattle and after service we were
having a potluck. I sat across from David. I could
not eat. I did eat, but it was very methodical and I
felt frozen in my seat, listening to him tell a story
about a monkey and a pole. As I was sitting there,
I felt a thread of light coming to me from David. I
felt so lifted up. I knew with my whole being that
I wanted to be in his presence, and to listen to his
stories and anything he chose to share.

The other memory I wanted to share is what
he told me at my Kriya ceremony:

"Kriya and Hong Sau are two very gentle and
very effective ways to reach Self-realization. The
Hong Sau is subtle but can produce very good
effects. Kriya, I have been doing for 35 years, and
each time it is a blessing, and is very effective.
These two things will help you most."

om sri ram jai ram jai jai ram om sri ram jai ram jai jai ram

MY MEETING OF DAVID was brief, although profound with lasting memory. There had been no intention nor knowledge of David until a spontaneous offer, by a friend, to meet and seek his support was suggested. It was as if unseen guidance had planned the details of travel and availability of all persons. A greater force propelled the experience, from the beginning of the original suggestion, to the meeting of David, to the unearthing of the true meaning of the experience that continues to unfold to this day! It is with humble gratitude that I have had the opportunity to meet and share sacred moments of truth with Yogacharya David. His parting words were "Love will always win. Place Love above all else."

om sri ram jai ram jai jai ram om sri ram jai ram jai jai ram

David hiking in Palm Desert, California, 2015

TRAVEL

AN AMERICAN SWAMI

IN JANUARY OF 2005 my 11-year-old son Jenrri and I were blessed to travel with David and Carla to Anandashram. Our excursion took us over the Pacific with a layover in Singapore, then on to a landing in Chennai on the eastern shore of southern India. We travelled at first like regular companions. I wrote about our day-by-day experiences in an article I wrote in March 2005 edition of The Cross and The Lotus Journal which includes several articles chronicling various aspects of this trip.

The profound turning point for me was seeing David through the eyes of Spiritual India and realizing the God-man he was in his own right. Our stay at Anandashram overlapped a visit by the saint Thuli Baba (photo page 5 of March 2005 Journal). David retells the "exam" questions Thuli Baba asked of him, beginning on page 4 of this journal. The conclusion at the end was the translator exclaiming for Baba, "He's got it!" Then this husky giant of a male devotee of Thuli Baba's (he made David look small by comparison) gave him a huge hug of congratulations.

It was an eye-opener for me to see David among a constellation of saints and that he was among the brightest. I'd gotten to know David simply as a friend and occasional hiking buddy. Here at Anandashram more than one Indian national arrived at the Anandashram gate with a little bit bewildered and embarrassed look, and just reporting they were inwardly directed to come and meet the "American Swami". No name, just a vision to guide them to our dear Davidji. It gave me a whole new perspective on just how much of a spiritual force David was, and grace to have so frequently had his darshan.

Other events etched in my memory are David reading "Stories by Swami Ramdas" to Swami Satchidananda at the entry steps with a crowd of about 100 people watching. Swamiji, David and Thuli Baba were seated side by side on the dais. David was bubbling with mirth and giving each story a full-throated dramatic reading! At each conclusion he would give his child-like smile and scrunch up his shoulders a little bit and give Swamiji a glance. All Swamiji would reply, with a broad smile, is "Another one". It was all great fun with peals of laughter and everyone lost in the moment.

The other poignant moment was when a group of about twenty-five Westerners passed through on their own tour of various Indian ashrams and heard about David and asked if he would come to their evening meeting and say a few words. The spiritual guide of the group did his best to inspire his followers with some opening remarks, but it came across like a dry textbook. David then shared some of his spiritual experiences and everyone immediately recognized he was speaking deep truths through his own experiences. At the conclusion of his talk the whole room felt uplifted and empowered by his divine wisdom and convinced that God-realization was obtainable.

I returned to my room with an over-arching thought of WOW! So blessed to have experienced David in his natural element with fresh eyes. I knew then what a supreme blessing it was to have David in my life. There was practical coaching when I was having a hard time coping, silly moments inspired by Papa's "where's the fun" and moreover pure bliss to have his darshan in this incarnation over and over and over again. Jai Guru, Jai Davidji!!

om sri ram jai ram jai jai ram om sri ram jai ram jai jai ram

AN UNEXPECTED BONUS while at Anandashram was the countless hours of darshan we had with David. Our rooms shared a porch, which meant we also shared tea-time, jokes, tears, visitors, laughter, sobs, sweets, and the gentle wisdom that flows from David like a river.

om sri ram jai ram jai jai ram om sri ram jai ram jai jai ram

WE TRAVELLED TO INDIA with David and a group of around eight people. We flew to London, spent the night, and then flew from London to Mumbai. When we got to Heathrow Airport for the Mumbai flight, there was a problem with overbooking and our check-in. I wasn't too concerned because, travelling with David, things always worked out. David talked to the agent and soon we had our boarding passes, with two of us in business class and the rest upgraded to a class with more spacious, more comfortable seats. Travelling with the guru had benefits!

When at Anandashram, everyone wanted to be with Swami Satchidananda, to be near him. People milled about, ready, in case Swamiji came out.

When Satchidananda did come out, a crowd would instantly gather. Swamiji would look around, saying "Where is David? Where is David?"

David would come forward, and a chair would be brought out for him. The two would sit together, sharing their Divine Companionship, surrounded by Swamiji's devotees.

om sri ram jai ram jai jai ram om sri ram jai ram jai jai ram

OBSERVING A GOD-MAN

FOR AROUND 7 YEARS or so, God blessed Ric and me with the most holy darshan of Yogacharya David and Carlaji, not only during services in centers in Washington, Oregon and various locations in British Columbia, including those wonderful retreats at Loon Lake, but during the winter months as well, when God has drawn His devotees to desert locations in California, Arizona and Utah. We sat around campfires together in the wide expanse of the Anza-Borrego Desert, toured a "living" underground cavern near Benson, Arizona, travelled to Master's Encinitas hermitage, hiked in places like Joshua Tree National Park, Sedona's Red Rock country, Indian Canyons on the outskirts of Palm Springs, and even through slot canyons, including one where ladders had to be climbed!

One evening, after a "cowboy dinner," we floated leisurely down the Colorado River in a huge aluminum jetboat, listening to great old songs like "Happy Trails to You," all the while being treated to an interesting and humorous commentary about the region by a local old-timer. So many "Ram adventures," as our Master David called them, our gratitude far exceeding any words that could ever come close to expressing it. All this being said, though, every single moment spent in our Master's loving and peace-filled Presence was a treasured gift, regardless of the setting.

Someone once asked me what it was like being with Yogacharya David during times like these, thinking perhaps that he would be different in some way, but without hesitation I could easily tell her, "He is the same." Always he was and is my Teacher, my Divine Friend, my Heavenly Father. Always he was and is Spirit, perfected. And I love him.

om sri ram jai ram jai jai ram om sri ram jai ram jai jai ram

LOON LAKE

MEDITATING WITH DAVID AT LOON LAKE

LOON LAKE RETREATS are some of my most treasured memories. It was an indescribable gift to be
in David's presence for those glorious long week-
ends, with beloved fellow devotees, surrounded
by clean calm forest beauty. Every single retreat I
went to was absolutely life changing. My favorite
part was the morning and evening meditation. It
felt like the greatest privilege to be in the room
with David while he sat silently indrawn in perfect communion with God. Of course, he was in
that state of communion with God all of the time.
But for me there was a unique and special power
and a rare blessing during those sacred silent
hours.

Davidji would usually come to the satsang
room around 5 a.m. I loved to watch the arati rit-
ual he would perform, which began with lighting a candle for each of the Gurus in turn: Jesus,
Babaji, Lahiri Mahasaya, Sri Yukteswarji, Master
and Mother. Next, he would light a new incense

stick and slowly wave the incense in a clockwise circle three times before each of the Guru's photos in turn, then in large circles to the four cardinal directions—North, East, South, West. The graceful movement of his hand finished each offering at the top of the third circle, with an extra lift of the incense stick to send the fragrant smoke heavenward. He ended by facing the altar and carefully placed the incense in its holder. He would reverently pronam to the Gurus, and then kneel down on the floor to bow completely. My heart heaved and tears came to my eyes every time I saw him bow down like that, in total surrender and devotion. Then he would settle into his chair, wrap his pale golden-colored shawl around his shoulders, arrange his legs either crossed or in half-lotus, turn his gaze upward and close his eyes, and quickly appear to be absorbed in an ineffable state of fathomless peace.

The atmosphere at that time seemed to me to be dancing with light, angels drew near and there was a thunderous joy that resounded and thrilled in every atom of the satsang room—radiating out to the world and beyond. I would keep my eyes open to look at him for some time, solidly fixing in my mind the cherished image of his meditating form. Then like a little child imitating a revered father, I would try to arrange myself like him, close my eyes and imagine I was with him where he was in the Universal Being of God. To sit with David during those precious moments was unforgettable. God was so close, I felt that by the slightest wisp of my love I could instantly touch the hem of His vast Being.

In the evenings, I tried to stay as long as possible at the end of the day's program—as long as David was there in the room. At the retreats I attended, on the first night, he would remain in meditation until after midnight. The following nights, it seemed God would prompt him to retire a little earlier, around 10:30 or 11 p.m. I found that if I was sleepy or my mind wandered during my attempts toward concentration, I could simply open my eyes and see David sitting right there before me, receive the uplifting currents emanating from his deep absorption in God and be refreshed and refocused to keep aspiring to the fullness I was capable of in the moment. Being in David's presence at that time felt like divine Grace was advancing my soul light years toward the goal of freedom in the realization of God as All and all in all.

I am so grateful for those cherished memories, especially now that David is no longer here in person. God lets me go back there with David in my mind anytime I am stale or struggling in my practice of meditation, to receive the blessing of refreshment. In my mind's eye, God beyond time brings me to that room at Loon Lake where I can see so clearly his beloved form sitting before me and feel so profoundly the emanation of love and pure divine consciousness that David ever is, and is ever One with. Such blessings! Such amazing, amazing blessings. Jai David. Jai Guru.

om sri ram jai ram jai jai ram om sri ram jai ram jai jai ram

SOME OF MY MOST CHERISHED memories of David are from the retreats. From the first ones in the summer at Phyllis's on Hornby, to finally settling to both spring and fall retreats at Loon Lake, they were always life changing. The powerful energy emanating from David, combined with so many like-minded souls together, was truly uplifting and transformative. The fact that the settings were beautiful and the food always good, was an added bonus.

om sri ram jai ram jai jai ram om sri ram jai ram jai jai ram

AT A LOON LAKE RETREAT, I was so grateful to have a moment together with David! I was sitting in an outside chair looking at the trees and basically just staring and wondering how blessed I was that

I was there, and absorbing all of the trees, the lake and the whole retreat. Absorb, absorb, absorb.

While sitting on said chair, David came out and sat with me. It felt so great, Great!! Together we looked out to the trees and lake and scenery . . .

He commented on a drawing I was working on, and I asked one question about helping others. He said to focus on the full potential of the person, see them not with the situation as it is and asking for help for them, but envision the person as whole, full of light and see them walking in the world fully and even dancing happily through the world. So that my well-intended thoughts hold the person in the needed state.

om sri ram jai ram jai jai ram om sri ram jai ram jai jai ram

I LOVED LOON LAKE with Davidji.

Arising before dawn, I would saunter down to the lakeshore to watch the otters playing in the emerald waters, as fish were rising to the surface of the lake. The tranquility was sublime.

On the ridges above, sun began illuminating the ridgetops.

I loved David's incredible themes for his workshops. Each one I attended contained powerful teachings, held in folders I still have, priceless in their wisdom.

Although an accomplished speaker, Davidji had a common touch, enabling those struggling, to suddenly be opened into the Light of God!

Many there I had never met before, yet we all held a kinship unequalled due to David's Universal Beneficence. He would often remark: Remain connected in "Spirit's Innernet". This was not using technology to go on Zoom-meetings... but to arise in Spirit.

om sri ram jai ram jai jai ram om sri ram jai ram jai jai ram

Viewing the Ganges at Rudraprayag, India, 2005

LESSONS

I LEARNED EARLY ON that everything David told me was true and his teachings helped me more than any others had ever done before. I listened and practiced what he preached, and time and time again, in each and every situation and complex predicament I got myself into, by doing what he taught, the results were ALWAYS better, resolved the issue, powerful and more "right" than anything I had ever tried and always failed before. It was such freedom and his help was so much better than anything my puny little brain could have ever conceived.

om sri ram jai ram jai jai ram om sri ram jai ram jai jai ram

I REMEMBER THE FIRST TIME I sat in front of David waiting for him to start talking. I remember saying to myself, "Is this the person who is going to answer my questions? Is what I have been looking for?" Can you imagine my delight when he started talking and it was like a warm waterfall of water washing over me.

One of the most important things David taught me, is that we have an inner voice of wisdom that we can tune into and listen to (the inner Guru) and that he was an outer Guru.

It wasn't only spiritual, David helped me with many practical things as well. I dislike paperwork, organizing and house-cleaning, I dislike calculating my finances. I have trouble organizing thoughts, and material things. David always said to me, you are here to learn how to navigate the practical world. I remember being exasperated and asking why? He looked at me and said, "Because you are here!" This makes me laugh because it is so obvious and to think that David had to put up with such a child. He did so with such patience and love. I am so grateful.

David modeled so many things. He was organized, on time with plans, well read, able to talk about so many subjects, and sociable. He was humble and would help others in every way, taking people's plates to the kitchen, for example, never acting like he was better than anyone else. He showed respect for everyone that he interacted with, even if he had to be firm and tell people off.

om sri ram jai ram jai jai ram om sri ram jai ram jai jai ram

DAVID HELPED ME during one of the toughest times of my life. The situation involved a small group of colleagues at work who began circulating false and hurtful rumors about me. It was clearly an attempt to get me to leave my job or even to get me fired. I had never experienced anything like this before and was caught off-guard by the sudden blow of oppositional force.

In the midst of my suffering, I came to David for help. He told me about a similar experience that he went through, albeit far worse than mine, and gave me tools for how to deal with what he called "psychic attacks." Simply having his complete understanding and empathy was wonderful, but he also reminded me of the power that we all have access to. He told me to stand firm in Truth, to feel that God and Gurus are standing strong with me, and that I am completely safe and protected, especially when in those higher states of consciousness. Of course, within days things felt very different at work, and within months it was transformed.

I am grateful to David for this and the many other times that he helped me. I am also grateful for the experience itself. Those individuals who opposed me ultimately gave me an opportunity to test out God's power, thereby increasing my faith and ability to handle whatever great dramas come my way. Oh, what fun.

om sri ram jai ram jai jai ram om sri ram jai ram jai jai ram

YOU HAVE A FRIEND IN GOD

I HAVE SO MANY good memories of David it's hard to narrow it down. He was a really good friend. He was calm, loyal, was up for adventure and had a great sense of humor. All the things you want in a friend—a great buddy—someone you looked forward to hanging out with.

But then there were these constant reminders that he was so much more.

David—in so many ways—was the voice of God. Devotees are often hung up on trying to figure out what God wants for them—or how they can tune into that spirit. But what's kind of ironic is God comes to us all the time every day—in the form of a dog loving you unconditionally—or a sunrise so beautiful your soul is lifted up—or even in a person acting so horribly you want to go to God so you never act that way. So, David—in so many ways—was that part of Himself that God sent to demonstrate Himself—to teach us things—to bring us closer to Him.

One time Carla and David came down for a few days so David could give a talk and do interviews. And it was always so exciting when they first showed up. I'd run out to their SUV and help unload and there was always so much stuff when you take your household and a Church on the road.

We'd all help bring in the harmonium and a few big suitcases and clothing on hangers. In the early days when all the kids were still at home and every bedroom was spoken for, they would stay out in our separate office building. It has its own shower, so they could be pretty comfortable and private.

We'd just gotten everything into the office. David was putting some things away and Carla and I were talking. I don't think she had ever been too crazy about the damp and cold Seattle weather, so we were talking about places they might like to go in the winter. This was a little while before their motorhomes and Arizona trips.

This is the kind of thing I love to do—strategize about your 'best life'. How can you arrange things to be as great as possible—and Carla and I were getting into it. "Oh, you could you leave at this time of year" I would say, "and then you could come back right when the rhodies and azaleas are blooming." And then Carla would talk about what she wanted and how it might work out and we were getting so excited about the prospects. And all through this animated and enthusiastic conversation David wasn't saying a thing. He was just quietly and calmly putting away clothing—getting situated for their stay.

So of course, I wanted to get him involved—after all, engineering your life to be the best it can be is so exciting. So I asked him, "David, if you could go anywhere and do anything, where would it be?"

And he calmly turned to me and said, "Wherever God wants me to go".

And THAT stopped me in my tracks. He said it with all humility—there was no rebuke there—just a big indication of where his consciousness was. And boy did it have an effect. I realized that spending more time trying to discern God's will for me might be better than putting so much effort into trying to steer the ship myself.

I immediately stopped that line of conversation and got more contemplative—and then got out of there to let them rest. But that comment really got me to thinking.

That was one of those times where David was the voice of God, delivered directly, clearly and with a powerful and important message. What's that worth in your life? And the answer might rightfully come back—*everything*.

om sri ram jai ram jai jai ram om sri ram jai ram jai jai ram

YOGACHARYA DAVID SAVED MY LIFE

ONE DAY GOD decided that it was time for me to have a fierce lesson: it was time for an intense Godward turn. Yes, my very life was on the line. Could I, would I, wake up? Did I have the capacity to avert a would-have-been-fatal car accident and the ability to deflect months of dark-force, astral attacks?

My good intentions and naivety set up the "test" or, a better word, "initiation." I had started a project with someone when I ought to have known better. Indeed, I had a gut-feeling warning about this person and an intuitive alert; still, I really wanted this particular project. However, thankfully, after a short time, I did wake up. The truth of what was really happening got through to my consciousness, and I listened. I ended the project and accepted responsibility for a bad decision on my part.

Was it over? No. The repercussions were resounding. I had angered a person who knew how to use energy in a dark and powerfully shadow-like manner. The hostile astral attacks began:

on my person, my energy field, and on my very way-of-being in general. Random. Week after week, for months.

I had read about such attacks, mainly from the Indian, Vedic literature and from some western literature as well. There are also other writings about these dark forces and how the creative spirit within can conquer them in mystical Christianity, the Kabbalah, Hawaiian Kahuna teachings, Buddhism and in many indigenous traditions.

I applied three rules:

Rule One: Stay calm and collected. When under an astral attack (dark-force energy) never fear, never get angry, never be in rage, and never blame . . . stay clear of all negative emotions. Negative emotions lower cognitive reasoning abilities; hence, people under the influence of these lower emotions have less reasoning power. They tend to make poor decisions. What is more, these negative emotions lower the body's frequency, thereby creating a downward gravitation to lower vibrations that tend to attract more low vibrations—a sure way to become a victim. As Yogacharya David reminds us, "Fear disconnects you from God; it builds fear upon fear and will dominate your life . . . you feel helplessly caught."[1]

---

1   Yogacharya David's quotes in this submission are from March and April *Discourses Volume Three 2016: A True New Birth.*

Rule Two: Stay aligned with one's highest light, and faith, and truth. In essence, to me, this means that we center ourselves in the soul-force of light and truth while keeping a centered alignment of light running through the body. This can be visualized by lighting up the central channel or the spinal channel that houses the chakra system. Then, anchor this alignment into the earth and upward into the highest cosmic consciousness, or godhead, or spiritual focus available, developed through previous practice. (If necessary, do this 24/7; teach the body-consciousness to assist you.)

Rule Three: Chant uplifting mantras or sacred japas (such as Aum) during and after all invasions of one's energy field. It is wise to have an uplifting spiritually-focused mantra, chant, or japa to call on at any time when challenged, or even to use in gratitude, as there is much to be grateful for in our lives.

Knowing that I was a novice in dealing with such stealth forces, I contacted my guru, Yogacharya David. I emailed him. I did not know what he would think about my odd situation. It did sound unusual and rather preposterous. Still, I trusted my guru would know that I was a reasonable person and that if I stated something, no matter how wild it sounded, he would give it credence. He did. He quickly responded, stating that he would be with me and support me through this ordeal.

I now, thankfully, knew that I had guru-support. Still, I kept my consciousness alert, vigilant, and available to recognize adverse intrusions. I realized also that, as comfortable as naivety is, and it is comfortable, it is just what predators want; it is what they play on, and what they use as a base for deception. (Note, for predators: fear, anger, greed, naivety, and ignorance—basically all negative emotions work for them.) Individuals can become captured or "charmed" and become reliant on the "other" deleting or dissipating their own truth, their own principles for living, and even their inner sacred soul-knowing: that is, allowing soul-sickness or soul-capture by others, or a dogma, or a narrative.[2]

On the other hand, we can accept a fierce lesson and see God's hand—God's Lila—as He has decided it is time for us to grow. It is rarely our choice, it is His! So, a harsh experience can become a major steppingstone—an

---

2   Yogacharya David has written about his astral attack experiences in his journals. See the book *Silence: Entering the Cosmic Sea of Consciousness*. Other descriptions are in his postings or discourses, available online or in his six volume book series.

initiation—into our next level of Christ-Krishna Consciousness.

Many months later, I saw Yogacharya David in person and thanked him. He responded: "I let you take all you could handle and I took the rest." We never spoke of this again. Yet, I know that while I did everything I knew to do, my spiritual warrior-self awake, Yogacharya David saved my life. He willingly, generously, and compassionately took the overload. And there was overload!

I will, indeed, always honor my great fortune. I have, even now, a master at my side, and a guru lineage of great masters.

I take seriously what Yogacharya David emphasized, to quote him: "My part is to willingly, full-heartedly, and mindfully, live each day as His instrument. That is all I can do, that is what He wants from me, and He will see to the rest...I am to remain connected to the all-important inner-net: the power and intelligence of Divine Consciousness." And, "We are all blessed beyond comprehension through our deepened connection with God-tuned beings—perfected in the fires of testing and blazing with the pure light of Divine Consciousness."

Om Davidji
Om Sri Ram Jai Ram Jai Jai Ram.

om sri ram jai ram jai jai ram om sri ram jai ram jai jai ram

THE LIFE OF A BHAKTA

I WANTED TO WRITE about an experience I had with my Guru. It was something that has occurred over a fairly long period of time and has given me the chance to see what it is meant by living the life of a bhakta. What I have seen very clearly in David is that he lives the life of a bhakta. He lives the life of Love. Love of God, family, friends, and everything around him. The example I want to share relates to what we all have to work with, and that's other people, other personalities in our lives that have, for some reason or another, caused us great harm, hurt, suffering, pain, sadness, anguish—the list goes on. For whatever reason, in this lifetime or some other time, a particular person comes into your life and it seems that every button that can be pushed, every negative strong emotion that you have is associated with this particular person. Sometimes it can even be a culture, religion, or any other number of things.

I was going through this experience very acutely and then quietly observed that a person that had at one time been present in David's soul's past had come back into his life. The person was not at the present time causing any difficulty but the awareness was there that at sometime the person had caused a great deal of suffering and pain in David's past life. I was also going through the similar kind of experience. However, my reaction was quite different than the one I was seeing and observing in David! In every situation that he was involved with this person, I saw only love, kindness, humor, warmth and sincere interest. I constantly watched for any thread of resentment, anger or even caution towards this person. I never saw or felt any, whatsoever.

I remember the story of Papa Ramdas. I recall reading that when Papa's daughter had passed away, a devotee watched closely for a week to notice any sign from Papa that would indicate his sadness or discomfort around this personal loss. Papa just continued to stay absorbed in his Love and Bliss for God; the connection with God never wavered, even during a time when most would be devastated when a beloved child passed away. I watched David for any deviation from his bhakti way; it just never happened. I have a strong intuitive sense and can see discomfort in others very clearly. I never felt or thought that David ever treated this person any differently than any other of God's children.

David has spoken in depth about the path of bhakti yoga and how he feels that being a bhakta is easier than a jnani. Loving God and seeing Him in everything is the way David lives every moment and it's the way I dedicate myself to being.

om sri ram jai ram jai jai ram om sri ram jai ram jai jai ram

A PILGRIMAGE IS such an opportunity to "change oneself" and it really has been a graduate school of learning on this tour. One example was at a campground we were staying: I was checking in at the office, and the park ranger, a middle-aged woman who was taking our fees, was unfriendly and harsh and never really looked at me. I was very surprised at her manner as I have found that all the other park rangers we have met were courteous and friendly.

David went with me the next time we went to make a change and he also observed the same attitude and behavior from her. After we had left, I mentioned that she had been this way with me the first time I met her. He said, "You really don't know what is going on with a person when they act that way, that there is something difficult or hard in their life." I remembered that he had said that before and knew the truth of his words.

As God directed this play, I had to go in to add another day to our stay there, and lo and behold, the same park ranger was there. Initially I thought, "Well, if she is harsh today, I'll just be harsh right back." Fortunately, I quickly realized how ridiculous that was and so I went to the counter and was pleasant and told her what I needed. She started to process the paperwork and while she was on the computer I thought about what David had said about her. I opened myself up to her and looked inside her and felt the words, "sad and lonely" come to mind. I quietly felt those feelings and held them to me in a warm blanket of love. All of a sudden, she looked up, smiled at me, handed the paperwork to me and spoke pleasantly and friendly. I was shocked and amazed! It was so incredible to see that transformation!

Going on this pilgrimage has changed me. I know so well the truth of Master's words, "Change yourself and you will change thousands."

om sri ram jai ram jai jai ram om sri ram jai ram jai jai ram

DAVID TAUGHT ME that I am very much a Jnani. In retrospect, it is amazing to think of how I approached some of the conversations with him. As he said a couple of times, I was a "tough customer." It's amazing now to think of things I said and asked. There were times I really "grilled" him. It became clear after some years on this path that my approach to learning the ultimate Truths, was/

is the same as how I navigated much of this life. My goal with David was that I wanted to know the highest Truth, only "God's Truth", please.

Even before Kriya initiation there was a conversation, as he was telling me something I should or should not do, in which I asked a certain question. I said something like, David, if I'm going to make these changes to my life, I want to know positively sure, that the instructions, advice, directions you are giving me are from God, not just human, good advice. I told him that I wasn't going to do this new life unless he could provide me assurances. And in that early conversation and a couple of times over the years, he confirmed the same fact. He told me that I could count on the fact that every word and action from him was the same as if it came directly from God. He made clear, there was no difference between his teachings and God's Truth. He literally told me, Rick, you now have me in your life, helping you to grow and learn, and everything from me is the same as if directly from God. (I am paraphrasing, of course).

We developed a fun bit of banter over the years about this. There were several times that he advised a certain action, to make a change, operate a certain way, and I would pause and say to him something such as . . . O.K. David, I just want to make sure that we still have the agreement that every word and action from you is the same as if it came directly from God, right? And he would usually grin and smile and say, Yes Rick, that's always correct.

And so from that as a foundation, with countless phone chats, emails, texts and meetings, my path was to ask him questions about general and specific topics. And he would tell me what God's Truth is. I am so incredibly grateful that he always kept responding to my questions, sometimes presented multiple times per week. (There were times that he did not respond at all, or some days or a week or two would pass, but that was uncommon and I did pretty well with accepting that was God's plan). He was so incredibly generous with his time.

Oh, he would occasionally tell me that God told him not to answer my question. And there were times that he would tell me to take some hours or days to pray, ponder, reflect and then we would reconnect, and he would tell me the answer, information or details I sought. And as years passed, often he would say to me, what do you think the Truth is and I will tell you if you have it correct, and if not, I'll tell you what part you have wrong.

I am so incredibly grateful to have had such opportunities with my Guru. I was the Jnani, intently, passionately seeking God's Truth and as he explained, God provided him for me to learn Truths from. And that, as a foundation, leads me to the following stories, each with a Truth that I was grateful to incorporate into my understanding and in some cases, would lead to making changes or adjustments to my life.

For months now, I have tried to get clear about if I am supposed to share certain stories or not. It seems that sharing some of these Truth-teachings is what I will do. And as he told me, if I try with all sincerity to do Right action and I don't do Right action, no Karma is incurred. David, I thank you forever.

POWERFUL MOMENTS

IT'S BEEN ABOUT TWENTY YEARS since I stepped consciously onto this path, with David as my Guru, guide and teacher. He has been my living example of "what would the Master do?" It has been amazing, and I feel incredibly blessed that in this lifetime God has provided me with much access and interactions with my Guru. With his guiding hand, this life is the greatest adventure!

Approximately ten years ago I was at a birthday party at our local bowling alley. One of the Schultz kids had a few friends gathered and a few adults were there too, including David and Carla. It was a busy day, somewhat loud and moderately chaotic. A lane or two away there was a family which included a middle-aged dad and a couple of grade-school kids. The dad was being harsh, negative and mean to his young son. Our group of adults and several kids were aware of this dad and his horrible interactions with his son. It was impossible not to notice or not to feel sad for this boy. Upon observing for some time, it was obvious that the dad thought this boy could simply do nothing right. The dad was loud enough to be disruptive to all in the vicinity. He had horrible body language, and what made me feel worst of all, several times he grabbed his son by his arm and directed him in such a hard way that I suppose most of us were thinking, "I hope he doesn't hurt his arm by pulling on it so aggressively."

It occurred to me that if David were not there, at some point I would have said or done something, but it felt clear to me that it was not my place to do anything. Not with David there. As I was bowling, I kept hoping (I suppose many others who were in the vicinity did as well) that this dad would stop. I began to wonder, what will David do? As time passed (it felt like 20 minutes, maybe it was only 5 or 10) and the scenario continued between the dad and son, it felt that each of the adults in our group were wondering the same thing: Surely David will do or say something—what will it be?

At one point, David very calmly took a couple of steps toward the area where this family was bowling, and he stood. Once again, this father acted out of line, over the top, certainly he was going well past any reasonable line of healthy parenting, reasonable reprimanding, or anything acceptable and fair to his son. Then David took a couple of steps into this man's "personal space" and what I saw was amazing. This dad faced David squarely in front of him; they were about three feet apart. It was as if this dad had entered into some receptive, subtle, trance-like mode. Their eyes were looking into each other's and the man was pretty calm. Earlier, I had anticipated that any comment from David would elicit an outburst from the man, but not now.

David made some brief comment to him. David was not speaking loudly and so I did not hear all of what he said. It was gentle. He did not exactly reprimand the man, he said something like: Sir, it seems that maybe you are having a bad day and possibly your son is experiencing the brunt of it. He went on to say something like: it seems that he is quite upset by this and it would be good if you were not so hard on him. The man was not resisting, not objecting, not defending himself at all. It seemed that the Truth of David's words had pierced directly into this man's heart and soul. His shoulders slumped, his face relaxed, and as I recall, it seems he said he was sorry to David and that David suggested that he apologize to his son, which he promptly and sincerely did. I suppose this interaction only lasted less than a minute. The man appeared changed, quite changed. David and the man exchanged some parting, gentle comments and David stepped back into our bowling area. No words were spoken between David and any of us about what had occurred. Everyone resumed their playing.

That man, his son and their other family members remained there, as did we, for another half hour or so. The man never did act poorly again, and it seemed that the man and his son were doing fine. I, and surely others in our group, had wondered, what will the Master do? We observed what a master could do. David brought pure love, calmness, peace and some words and tone that seemed absolutely perfect for this dad to hear and feel. As I left the bowling alley and went home it occurred to me that David's comments and his Shakti power improved that man and his son's relationship forever. I believe it did.

DOGS

THERE WAS A PERIOD around two years when I was routinely experiencing a specific type of psychic circumstance regarding dogs that had died, apparently from vehicles having hit them. These dogs would be alongside of various small or large roads. David and I talked a lot about this as months passed and incidents occurred. His general guidance was this: he said that the souls of these dogs needed something and were reaching out to me for it. He directed me to always do my best to focus my God-energy on those dogs until the feeling subsided. Sometimes it would last for a few seconds and other times for a minute or more. Occasionally I would pull over, as David had advised was sometimes needed. At other times I would keep driving.

During the couple of years that these experiences were occurring, usually it was times when deceased dogs were alongside roads, but occasionally there were other occurrences. One day I was walking in the middle of the day in my neighborhood in the Medford area. I was walking on one side of the two-lane neighborhood road and I noticed that, from approximately 100 yards away coming toward me on the other side of the road, there was a man walking a very athletic, medium sized dog. It was on a leash. As we got closer to each other, there was a very strong, terrible feeling that came over me. It was similar to the feelings with dogs alongside roads, but different. And so, I did what David had told me to do. I slowed my walk to nearly being stopped and did my best to focus God-energy on this dog.

As we got closer to passing each other (as we were walking opposite directions) this dog looked at me with anguish, as if to beg me to please help it. Its owner was being mean to it, smacking it, pulling it very hard by its leash, talking very mean to it. In that moment I felt the urge to do more than I was already doing. It occurred to me to possibly confront the man, or to try to use psychic power to affect the situation. But David had made me promise, years earlier, that I would never try to use any "powers" to affect anything, unless he had instructed me to do something, as he had regarding the deceased dogs. And so, as much as I felt so sad for this seemingly abused dog, I kept walking. As I walked, the very strong feelings faded. Within 10–15 minutes I got to my home. That incident had so much energy in it that I thought about it several times in the coming hours and days.

About a week passed before I had my next conversation with David. (For 10–15 years we talked often, sometimes more than once per week, rarely going more than a few weeks between chats.) When we talked, I told him the story. Amazingly, as often happened, he told me that he was "with me" when that story occurred. He said that I did the right thing, by focusing my God-energy on the dog, and also by resisting the urge/desire to try to do anything further. And he added a comment that was so sad and yet profound. He told me that the soul of that dog had karma that it needed to work through and that being owned by this abusive man was accomplishing the process that was needed. It was a hard truth to hear.

This was one of many experiences that occurred for me regarding dogs. David talked with me about many of the stories that unfolded. That chapter of my path with David lasted about two years. I have not had a dog incident of apparent God nature for the past 6–8 years.

WEEDING

SOME YEARS AGO David and Carla were in one of the stages of doing improvement projects on their Mount Vernon house. David had created an invitation/request for devotees to come on some particular day to do a lot of weeding and groundskeeping. Many devotees participated and much was accomplished. The truth for me, which is not fun to acknowledge but it is the truth, was that some part of me, my interior voice said, "Ahh, I'm so glad I don't live nearby," because then I wouldn't have a good excuse for not being there!

You see, I absolutely HATE weeding. Possibly it's because my parents demanded that I do that a lot as a kid? Well, my truth is that as an adult, I have gone to great lengths to either avoid having residences that required such care, or to have enough funds to pay someone to do it, and mowing, and planting, etc. The bottom line is that I've been supporting myself with full time income, pretty much since I was about 16. And I've rarely ever done any of this kind of tasks/chores/efforts. Almost none.

A few years then passed, following that Mount Vernon event. My story occurs on the weekend of Terry and I getting married at David and Carla's house on Camano Island. I think I was doing pretty well with not having much ego about this being my/our weekend, but it seems David had a lesson for me to experience. Yep, I was generally able to see the humor and profundity in it at the time. But over time I have realized it even more.

Either the day before our wedding, or possibly the morning of it, my question for David was to the effect of "Is there anything else you would like for me to do to help get ready for our wedding?" Well, much to my shock, and possibly horror, he mentioned the "W" word, in relation to me no less! Lol. What is the "W" word, you ask? That word would be. . . . weeding! Oh, the horror! I HATE weeding!

He very casually walked me out to the area of gravel between their landscaping and the street. He said that Carla had asked that someone remove the weeds from that area, approximately 8 x 75 feet. I have chuckled to myself since then when I think about it. Oh my gosh, it was MY wedding weekend and I was being asked to do something that is one the things in life that I have very carefully avoided, successfully causing myself nearly zero weeding in my entire adult life.

I've paid for weeding and had women partners who have done it (possibly even enjoying it?!). And at times I've eliminated the need for such things, by methods such as ground cloth, cement, rocks, etc. And there I was, not only being asked to do weeding, on MY wedding weekend, but it was sort of hot (I don't like being hot) and the weeds were tiny (another thing I don't like), hard to remove, etc. But of course, my Guru was asking me to do this, and so of course I did.

It seemed like it took many hours. (But was it?) In reality, it probably took no more than 2 hours. As I did the weeding, I did everything I could to make the most of it. I did Om Sri Ram and thought about God things, and tried to hear some music from down the street. Finally, that task was done. Frankly, it felt great to have done it and I was also sooo darn happy to be done with it. And then as I was putting away the weeding tools in the garage, David "just happened" to appear in the garage during those brief couple of minutes. I was aware that it seemed like we were in some sort of cocoon of privacy, just he and I, not to be interrupted by anyone or anything.

Frankly, there was a part of me that was just hoping upon all hope that there was no more weeding to do! And so I (cautiously) asked David "Is there anything else you would like me to do?" I was sooo much hoping that he would not say the "W" word again! Well, he did, but in the best possible way. He sort of grinned and said something such as "Well, there is no more weeding to do." He looked at me in a special, somewhat piercing, Guru-like way as he said it.

I realized in that moment that he was definitely up to something. And so I fessed up! I told him, with tears in my eyes and very choked up, that I was so sorry that a few years earlier I had used distance as an excuse for not being at the group project. I told him that I was so sorry, but that I absolutely hate weeding and such activities and that although I wanted to want to be there back then, I just couldn't get past the fact that I hated such chores. I went on for a couple of minutes, emotionally telling my truth. And he stood there listening with his amazing, calm focus, as if no other situation existed in the world at that moment. He had a subtle grin on his divine face the whole time.

I made some comment like, isn't it interesting that Carla wanted weeding done today and that you asked me, not someone else? He smiled a big smile. And he said something like, you created some karma by not helping with that project back then. Isn't it great that Carla had a chore that gave you the opportunity to take care of that karma? I said that it seemed he may have had something to do with this, and he just smiled. And I made a comment such as, well, I suppose that's not an instant karma process, as it took a few years, but it seems to be something like that. I made that comment with a question mark tone. He smiled bigger and said something like "Yes Rick, always remember that God is involved in everything, even the weeding." It hit me and I cried and was blessed to share a big hug with him. And then he commented, such as, there's nothing else that you need to do now. That's all there is for you to do. Thank you for weeding. And then we both exited through separate doorways out of the garage.

What a profound experience that was. It was such an opportunity to see how the Master, my Guru, was somehow involved in all aspects of my life, from the seemingly most profound subjects to the most mundane.

Thank you so much for that experience and lesson, David.

Om Sri Ram Jai Ram Jai Jai Ram.

om sri ram jai ram jai jai ram om sri ram jai ram jai jai ram

CHANTING RAM NAM SILENTLY, INWARDLY, AS INSPIRED BY DAVID

LONG AGO I STARTED chanting Ram Nam regularly. I started with Ramdas's Ram Nam as they used to have it in Ramdas's own voice on the Anandashram web site. I have also chanted Ram Nam with Master's chants. My favourite of Master's currently is "Who tells me Thou art dark, oh my Mother Divine?" I like to think that those two Masters (Ramdas and Master Yogananda) injected some extra spiritual "zest" into their chants, and being a little bit greedy for God...well, why not benefit from that extra spiritual energy?

So, I chant those chants as I learned them, enjoying the extra spiritual charge.

I then started chanting Ram Nam when out walking. I found it adjusted itself to my pace of walking and I also found at rest that the pace and the cadence of Ram Nam regularly adjusted itself to my heartbeat. (How neat is that?)

Then I discovered that if I had an "ear worm" going around and around in my head, chanting Ram Nam would almost immediately clear it up/transmute it for me. Ramdas has <u>never</u> failed me yet in clearing up that "ear worm" condition!

I was comparing notes with David on this topic once a number of years ago. He said that he does the same thing to cancel out ear worms. And in that conversation, he also said that he chanted Ram Nam quietly, inwardly wherever and whenever he had the chance.

Inspired by David, I started to do the same in all circumstances, even while working, and have continued with the practice over the years. (NB: I do pay close attention when driving my car as I don't want to injure or, worst-case scenario, kill anyone with my car.)

om sri ram jai ram jai jai ram om sri ram jai ram jai jai ram

PEANUT BUTTER

ONE OF MY FIRST small lessons given me by my guru was during a sunny breakfast gathering at George and Christine's house in Maple Ridge. I believe it was my first visit for the rapturous carol singing and Christmas service that was so generously held there for the group.

It was the morning after the divine singing and we were happily filling our plates and drinking in the bliss of being in David's pure company. My thoughts suddenly turned to the different condiments on the table...almond butter, peanut butter, etc. "Ugh, I would never eat that kind of peanut butter, full of sugar and chemicals, and who knows what else. So unhealthy." So went my untrained mind.

David suddenly looked right at me from across and down the table and said loudly and clearly, "Would you please pass the peanut butter?" His smile was radiant. I quickly passed the jar as my whole being instantly felt drenched in shame. My cheeks burned. At the same time, I felt deep down the correctness of the lesson, and was thrilled to experience this care and attention from such a great one. It was the first time in my life that the shame of making a mistake did not take all power, for the total Love of my guru was washing over me throughout.

When I look back at this memory I am filled with such gratitude for my guru, and tenderness for that poor, yet incredibly blessed little devotee who had so much to learn—and still does! O what I would give for David in his human form to come and admonish me daily in every way needed. Om Guru Om.

om sri ram jai ram jai jai ram om sri ram jai ram jai jai ram

WHEN DAVID CAME to Vancouver B.C., he would see people for appointments. I felt greedy because the minute I got word that he was taking appointments I would call and book myself in. I told David I felt greedy and that I was concerned that other people needed a session that I was jumping in to take. He asked me to leave that decision with him. That was very freeing for me.

I also have a problem getting places on time. I was late now and then for David (maybe more than now and then). One time David told me not to be late again. I shared with him how much shame I have about being late and I told him that I was mortified that I had to be told off by him. To this day my heart remembers his loving response.

He looked at me as if he deeply took in what I had said (which he did) and he lovingly said, "I will remember that". I felt heard and seen and cared for by him. I was rarely late for an appointment again.

om sri ram jai ram jai jai ram om sri ram jai ram jai jai ram

MANY YEARS AGO, David and I were headed somewhere in his older stick-shift truck. I was lamenting about what a shameful, worthless person I was, so far from the goal, so unworthy. Shifting the truck into a lower gear as we began to mount a hill, he challenged me. "So, you are arrogant enough to think that you are too big to be contained in the all-ness of God?"

om sri ram jai ram jai jai ram om sri ram jai ram jai jai ram

DAVIDJI'S GREATEST GIFT to me was that he allowed me to watch him transition from son of man to son of God, and convinced me, that I too (and anyone reading this) could find my realization in this lifetime.

om sri ram jai ram jai jai ram om sri ram jai ram jai jai ram

IT'S JUST THE BEGINNING

AT EVERY TALK and workshop that David teaches, something new is brought forth to my consciousness that feels like a light being turned on in that ever-present dark room. Through God and Gurus' grace I am so privileged to be able to attend all that David teaches and there is not any program that has not benefited me in ways too numerous to mention.

One such occasion happened during the first talk he gave after the New Year. I never have any idea what God is going to show me that will get me closer to Him, and it's always interesting to see how it all evolves. In the course of David's talk, he said that God-realization is "not the end, but the beginning." It was as if some lightning crack knocked me awake to such a profound Truth.

I know that part of me, that ego-driven self, always had in the back of my mind that once I got the realization of my Oneness with God, that was the end; all would be over for me. Obviously that brought forth feelings of fear of the unknown: "What the heck would happen to me, where would I go, what would I do, would I be in this black void of nothingness?" There was a sensible part of me that knew that God-realization was

something that would free me from all this suffering, but just exactly what would happen?

When David said those words, that it was "the
beginning, not the end," then for the first time I
felt this sense of relief and freedom! Getting realization was truly the beginning of who I truly am,
that it's the beginning of knowing that I really am
a child of God, that God does love me, and that as
Mother said, "I know that I know." That's when
the really fun adventure begins—knowing completely without any doubt. Conventional wisdom
says that once you finish one goal, you start on
another. Well, I don't really see God-realization
as some kind of goal, it's more like the beginning
of who I truly am in God, and that is what I want
more than anything else!

om sri ram jai ram jai jai ram om sri ram jai ram jai jai ram

DAVID AS COUNSELOR

PART OF MY PROFESSIONAL background was being involved and working with therapists in the mental health field as well as working with them personally. I was very familiar with many therapists and that burnout was common in such a demanding and stressful field. After about a year of attending David's talks and working with him individually on my own emotional and spiritual development, it came to me so clearly that "David's well would never run dry". His spiritual connection and pipeline to God was solid and permanent. I knew, without a shadow of doubt that he had access to the Creator of all Creations and that his flow would never run dry or that he would ever "burn out". His Source was All in All and that was quite a comfort, revelation and really, amazing to me to witness. His help was practical, supportive, inciteful and most importantly, full of love—I knew it came from God.

om sri ram jai ram jai jai ram om sri ram jai ram jai jai ram

I saw David for a brief time while he was working as a counselor and mediator. His bliss as he brought people together was soothing. In private, however, he told me of a battle he was having with walls within himself.

Years later, after Mother left the body, I began going to services led by David. At times I saw his form in utmost repose, radiating light. Once in a private session with him he suggested I get close with my inner child, and afterwards when I went to David's service I felt a burst of childlike joy— the child of God! Another time, David had a workshop on meditation and after this time with him I had an experience of absolute worthiness—I could easily deserve to win the lottery, with this feeling.

om sri ram jai ram jai jai ram om sri ram jai ram jai jai ram

Hard to put into words all the help and support and guidance I received from David. What can I even begin to say about David? Words fail me; what I know is that he saved me from myself.

I knew David for approximately 20 years on this earth. What I carry with me from David is his love, support and the desire to be always doing my best for God in whatever form. I fail so many times but David prompts me back. Whenever I did something that was not well thought out with David, my shame was burning. I just did not want those things to happen again!

David's compassion was always evident and he gave me what was needed to grow in God and I must keep this uppermost in my life.

Om Davidji

om sri ram jai ram jai jai ram om sri ram jai ram jai jai ram

MY JOURNEY WITH DAVID started shortly after I had lost my second child who had been born full term at the healthy weight of 10 pounds. My son Sean died after 18 days from a genetic syndrome which affected his lungs. I knew right away that I wanted to try for another child in the future, but I had a 25 percent chance that any further children would have this genetic syndrome.

David is the person who stood out as being the main person who I could talk to about this. I will always remember the love he had coming out of him that was so kind and supportive whenever I said I wanted to try again. He lovingly said that souls line up to come and have this very special experience on earth. I remember him reflecting on how wonderful babies are with such love in his heart and his eyes.

When I told him that I was pregnant again, I do remember seeing shock on his face. Next time I saw him, he had checked in with God and God had told him everything was going to be OK. He seemed to not be shocked anymore; he told me he was very happy for me.

In September 1999 I gave birth to a healthy baby girl. I took her with me to so many of David's talks and to my Kriya initiation at the Unity Church in Seattle. Michelle would have been about six months to a year old at the initiation. David said to me shortly after Michelle's birth, "Childbirth is painful, hey?" I said, "How do you know?" He said," I felt some of your pain when you were going through your childbirth with Michelle."

Although I did not understand fully at the time, David's ability of tuning into God's will had him saying and doing all the right things to assist me in coming to understand myself better. David was and still is a huge support and teacher in my life. David was the kind of person who was always there at the right time, a Guru who listened as much as he spoke.

om sri ram jai ram jai jai ram om sri ram jai ram jai jai ram

DAVID COULD TAKE a person from a horrible inner crisis to being so uplifted in a short time. If things happen now, I hear David in my head and heart and am able to work though it as if he is right here. A benefit of not living close to David is that the majority of my communication has been in prayer and the answers come in meditation. It is likewise now. My Guru is my Guru always.

om sri ram jai ram jai jai ram om sri ram jai ram jai jai ram

David and Carla at Glacier National Park, Montana, 2016

Both Human
and Divine

CHRISTMAS TOYS

DAVID LOVED CHRISTMAS. How truly he understood the deep subtle mysteries, the profound
spiritual significance of the birth of Christ into
the world. He also celebrated all the joyful holi-
day traditions to the fullest. He was an avid dec-
orator for the season. He sought far and wide for
the perfect creche scene to display on the mantle
at his and Carla's Camano Island home. He was
among the first in the neighborhood to get those
neat laser projector lights, so the whole front of
his house was dancing with colorful twinkles.

Most memorable and charming was his
delight in cute stuffed-animal singing Christmas
toys. I had the blessing of being at David and
Carla's house for three Christmas events. At the
first event, David had a trio of stuffed farm animals—a dog, pig and cow—dressed as carol-
ers, which played the tune of Jingle Bells with a

woof, oink and moo. The next year introduced a plush moose who sang a rendition of the classic song, with his own special lyrics: "We wish you a Merry Christ-moose and a Happy New Deer!" The third Christmas, a cuddly singing Rudolph made his debut and stole the show, being a toy that could dance in circles on his hind legs while singing his featured tune, "Rudolph the Red-Nosed Reindeer." David would show the talented toys to visitors—adults and kids—with laughter and undiminished entertainment every time. The toys were cute, but what I really loved was how sweet and fun David was, and how he genuinely got a kick out of them. David used to say that fun is one of the most underrated qualities of God, and a good one to remember. God in David was certainly full of laughter, joy and fun!

om sri ram jai ram jai jai ram om sri ram jai ram jai jai ram

CHRISTMAS WELCOME

I HAVE A STRONG MEMORY of visiting David and Carla at Christmas time. They were hosting a Christmas carol sing at their home.

We arrived after dark, following a long drive. Their home glowed with candy cane lights down the driveway, a large Japanese maple with white lights, a wreath on the door. As we came up the front stairs, the door opened, revealing the warmth and light inside. David came to the door, with his soft chuckle, arms opening for a welcoming hug.

I imagine when this lifetime of mine comes to a close, David will be there, in the warmth and light, arms open, chuckling softly, welcoming me in.

om sri ram jai ram jai jai ram om sri ram jai ram jai jai ram

VERY SOLITARY BY NATURE, Christmastime always brings forth the desire to sing as I did when a child at our Seattle parish Church.

My memory of David was his Enthusiasm over bringing all devotees together to sing Christmas carols, with an accomplished concert-pianist to accompany their voices. Wonderful song books were created with lyrics of commercial tunes for children, leading to sacred carols, such as "O Holy Night."

Many years this took place, despite devotees and the pianist traveling through harrowing winter storms and expenses to gather together in God's Presence.

I will never forget this as long as I live!

om sri ram jai ram jai jai ram om sri ram jai ram jai jai ram

WAFFLE SATURDAY

DAVID HAD A TRADITION of making waffles for breakfast on Saturday mornings. One weekend, I was invited to come to David and Carla's house for Waffle Saturday. Carla had gone out on errands. She was very mindful of how precious time with David was for each and every devotee and would retire from the room when God directed so others could have the benefit of time alone with him. But David was sure to make a waffle for Carla and keep it aside for when she got home.

I was relatively new to having any one-on-one time with David. The predominant feeling I had for him was one of utter awe and reverence for the unfathomable presence of God in him, along with infinite gratitude for receiving me as a disciple. Whenever I was near him, my whole nervous system felt like it was plugged into a million-megawatt electrical power station, at the maximum amperage it could withstand—plus ten percent. He was always so compassionate, gentle, funny, down-to-earth, easy—the embodiment of pure love. Equally at the same time, just behind the surface of his human form, was radiating the Absolute Power, the Divine Force, the Will, the Consciousness that creates and sustains and destroys all worlds. I marveled to see this divinely perfected, Universally-realized master, standing at the kitchen island, wearing a colorful striped apron, joyfully telling me about the day he discovered that adding sparkling water to the batter makes waffles extra fluffy.

I sat at the dining table in a state of adoration and awe, doing my best to surrender my self-consciousness and talk with David as I watched him cook. He asked how many waffles I would like, would I prefer butter or coconut oil, syrup or jam, did I want any tea or coffee—so sweetly and thoughtfully he served me my waffles first, then brought his own and sat at the table with me for breakfast. He conversed so naturally, flowing seamlessly from things esoteric to ordinary. I think he understood this was a new and bewildering experience for me, being in his presence in such a personal way. He was all love and kindness, and his easiness made it possible for me to relax just enough to enjoy the delicious waffles he had expertly prepared.

Though I could not comprehend it all at the time, everything David talked about that morning was perfect for what I needed as a soul. To this day, I am still absorbing the Grace and the lessons he was imparting. Even beyond the blessing of listening to his wisdom, God in him was teaching me, blessing me, healing me, awakening me on every level of my being. The privilege of having that special time with David showed me that the

Guru serves the devotees so tenderly and humbly, and serves all humanity so selflessly, sparing no concern for themselves—and in so doing, melts the boundaries of ego into all-surrendering pure Divine Love.

om sri ram jai ram jai jai ram om sri ram jai ram jai jai ram

I REMEMBER DAVID in golden sunlight at Grandma's Farm,* spinning us kids around and throwing us into the air amidst apple trees in the orchard, laughing one and all. I remember Sunday School God-walks, down to Matthews Beach on Lake Washington, or through the hole in the fence behind the Seattle Congregational Church where Mother's group met after outgrowing my grandma's home, again walking down to the lake. David and other Sunday School teachers provided snacks—donuts for us and stale bread for the hungry ducks. David pushed us so high on playground swings there, I felt we could fly right off, up and away. I couldn't know then that he would one day push my soul to do just that!

Even better than play time and God-walks were guided meditations in the quiet of the basement of the church. We would lay down with eyes closed and David's soft, baritone voice would transport our restless minds to stillness and light.

He would lead us down a staircase or up a ladder, with each step or rung quieting, expanding, lightening our minds, then leaving the physical and mental to rest and merging into Light. Pure. Bliss. I never wanted those journeys to end, never wanted to leave David's steady, guiding voice. That feeling—pure love and calm while basking in the sound of David's voice and presence never left.

As an adult, after David became my own gurudeva, he walked me out to my car after a service in his and Carla's Camano Island home. When I raised my eyes to meet his own, I was staring at pure, golden light. Physical features were secondary to the brilliance emanating all around his form. How can I possibly describe who and what our gurudeva is? Words do not suffice. I crumbled to the dust of my guru's feet in that moment, and will be forever content to be just that. Just that.

---

* Rustic, waterfront property in south Puget Sound, owned by Bonnie Barnowe's family. Annual church campouts were held here in the 1980s.

om sri ram jai ram jai jai ram om sri ram jai ram jai jai ram

FOR ME DAVID has always been an ordinary man. The one thing he did that so very few have done, is he never gave up his spiritual practice. He was glued to Mother and her teachings. For that dedication he became a not so ordinary man.

It was interesting for me to watch how each person who stood before David thought in that moment of time that they were the ONLY person in David's life and how David projected that idea.

Jerry and I watched him grow very comfortably into those very big shoes Mother left for him to fill. We watched him leave his body and those very big shoes were once again left behind for others to fill.

I stand in awe of God's working with all His children and how all His plans manifest into perfection. David was for sure that perfection manifested.

How we all miss him.

om sri ram jai ram jai jai ram om sri ram jai ram jai jai ram

I FIRST MET Yogacharya David Hickenbottom in September of 1994. I had taken a couple of Reiki classes led by Phyllis Victory in Prince Rupert, B.C. She said that she was going to have a meditation at her home in Vancouver, B.C. and my husband and I were able to attend. After the meditation Phyllis introduced me to David, and he spent about 20 minutes with me.

Connie Meisner and myself would meet at Connie's home every Sunday and listen to talks that David had made on CD. There were 3 or 4 individuals sometimes. We then decided to invite David and Carla to Prince Rupert. At times David would also have classes with specific topics. I attended all of these classes. I had private sessions at each visit to Prince Rupert. I found the information very helpful and knew I wanted to continue on this Path. Gradually other individuals would join the group.

I felt that David had real and spiritual knowledge. He had softness in what he taught. If he wanted to convey something he would sometimes be firm. He would always have some humorous stories to share.

I would like to mention what would happen sometimes when Connie and I would listen to the CD. She would listen to the CD before our meeting. When I arrived she would start the CD and it would not play. It did eventually. There was obviously something 'electrical' going on.

David did initiation of Kriya Yoga to the Prince Rupert group and some devotees of Mother and

David also came to Prince Rupert for this event. It was a very profound experience. David also taught Master's Lessons to our group.

I had many telephone calls with David about my situation. I had been having some symptoms in the body that were disturbing. He guided me and explained what was happening and how to assist the process. Although David has now left the body, as I am experiencing various symptoms, I recall his words and my times with him continues to be very valuable. He helped me through my fear.

In 2005, my husband and I moved to Victoria. He and Carla would often travel to Victoria. He would teach classes and give talks. I attended all these classes. I also went to Maple Ridge several times for retreats. I attended the weekly meditations at John and Dianne's home. When they retired as centre leaders, Maureen Chlopan became the centre leader. We continue to attend service on Sunday mornings and listen to talks by David and Mother.

When David was in silence for the year, I would write my questions and send them to him. He would respond in writing. I was so pleased that I could continue my guidance from him during the year.

I enjoy the knowledge being produced in book form now.

I will always be very grateful to David and Carla for their work.

om sri ram jai ram jai jai ram om sri ram jai ram jai jai ram

I MET YOGACHARYA David Hickenbottom during the week of my first Kriya Yoga initiation in 1980. During the week of Kriya, there were a number of events, one of which was a talent show in someone's home. A variety of gifted devotees performed dance, music, and other offerings. David and his wife at the time, sitting perpendicular to me, were so warm and welcoming, beaming great smiles at me (the new country belle) throughout the show. I was delighted with my apparent welcoming into the fold.

Over the next few years, I was able to meet with David a couple of times. The next Christmas, I had the privilege of staying in David's family home where I enjoyed their heart-warming hospitality of the season. A year or two later, Mother had sent David to give a service at our Victoria chapel. Following his service, we visited together in an outdoor courtyard. While gazing into his brilliant eyes, I felt transported into the Divine

Consciousness that he was emanating. I was awe-struck to sense that he was far along toward his full realization. This darshan carried me throughout many months.

Years later, after returning home from several years of working and traveling abroad, I began attending services at the home of John and Dianne Durkin, our most gracious Center leaders. It was then that I began seeing David during his Victoria visits, a joyous rediscovery.

A couple of years later, David asked me to become the new Center leader for Victoria, which was the greatest honour I could possibly have imagined. Feeling overwhelmed with gratitude, of course my answer was YES. This meant that I would host him and Carla during their future visits. That would involve his counselling sessions with various devotees in my living room, meal sharing, walks in the neighbourhood, and of course Sunday service and a potluck shared among a houseful of people—Kriyabans, friends, and neighbours here to celebrate darshan from our Divine David.

He was extraordinarily appreciative and thankful during our farewell rituals. And upon his departure, he left enormous blessings and God vibrations with me in my home to bask in for weeks following. And his final farewell was in no terms final. He left a wealth of teachings and is as fully alive as he ever was.

om sri ram jai ram jai jai ram om sri ram jai ram jai jai ram

IT WAS ALWAYS a great gift to serve David and Carla in their homes in whatever way I could. Carla is such a gracious hostess, and David's unending patience and generosity not only healed me, but provided a wonderful example of how I wanted to be, what I could strive for. Such wonderful memories will remain in my heart forever.

om sri ram jai ram jai jai ram om sri ram jai ram jai jai ram

THE MEMORY I'D LIKE to share happened in 2017 on "the day after Christmas, but in February," Yogacharya David's birthday! I heard him once refer to this time in his life as the "birthday season," most likely, I imagine, because of the constant flow of thoughtful gifts and sincere wishes that invariably came his way each year on that day. Reverend Larry Koler and his wife Cate had flown down to California to visit their fellow Kriyabans and longtime friends, and to honor David on this special occasion. We, (husband Ric and I) in our travel trailer, and David and Carla in theirs—our "Dharamshalas on wheels," as David used to call them—were camping in a quiet, idyllic spot on Lake Cahuilla on the outskirts of La Quinta at that time.

By the way, you may not know that our dearest Master David had given a name to each of his two RVs, affectionately referring to the first one, a Bigfoot Class C, as "Hanuman Bigs," and the second one, a Class A motorhome, as "Ganapati Jai." Ganapati is another name given to the revered Hindu deity, Ganesha, the elephant.

Mid-morning on the 26th of February, our party of six left Lake Cahuilla and drove to Palm Springs, then stepped into an aerial tramway and were transported up to the top of Mt. San Jacinto where we were to enjoy lunch together. As we walked to our table, I remember turning to Reverend Larry and asking him if we should fill this time with reminiscences of Mother Hamilton, our Guru. Sure enough, that's exactly what God had ordained for us that afternoon. In the evening we gathered together again, this time in David and Carla's RV, to share birthday cake. I had purchased a gluten-free flour that I'd never baked with before but was optimistic that it wouldn't present any problem. But it did! While the others waited and waited for me to arrive with the cake, I was very busy tweaking it, adding a bit of this, trying a bit of that, and a bit more of this to it. I had placed tiny photos of Mother on top of the cake, so was satisfied with the decorating, but it seemed like this cake just wasn't going to be moist enough.

Unnoticed by the others, I arrived on the scene a bit frazzled. As I sat down beside my peaceful Teacher, I inwardly let go of the tension I was holding. **In that very instant**, Davidji ever so quietly uttered, "mmm."

I presented Davidji with two small gifts that evening. One of them was a children's book. I had spotted him slowly turning the pages of this book in a giftshop the previous day when we'd all visited and hiked a bit on the Palm Canyon Trail in Indian Canyons, also known as Tahquitz Canyon. This particular trail was also blessed by Mother, who visited this area back in the late 1950s, I believe it was. Indeed, this truly is a sacred spot.

The other gift I gave my beautiful Teacher that day was actually something he'd suggested I give him, in an email to me a few days before. In the subject line of this email were these words: "If I may be so bold . . . " Needless to say, I was more than happy to have received this suggestion and got busy creating it for him. He'd asked me to write out the following words by Papa Ramdas for him, which soon after I saw hanging on the wall in his RV:

"Let the house thrill with the sound of God's
Name and Glory.
In such a house, the spiritual atmosphere
will always have a favourable reaction
On the health of the inmates, both physical
and mental.
Love flows there in floods."

It's not easy writing about one of THE most
incredible souls EVER to have crossed one's path!
Jai Davidji! Jai Mother!

om sri ram jai ram jai jai ram om sri ram jai ram jai jai ram

GOD IS FUN

I RECENTLY HAD A DREAM of David I want to share
with you. I had listened to the talk David gave
immediately after he came out of his silence at
Cloud Mountain. The talk had uplifted me, and
I was reminded as to how much of a sense of
humor he had and the different ways that would
show up.

The setting of my dream was a big, unfamiliar
house. It was a gathering of devotees and only
some of them were familiar to me and many were
not. It was a very informal, casual setting and
David was roaming among the devotees, having
miscellaneous conversations. At times he would

get everyone's attention, teach a brief lesson or make a comment, and then the casual flow would continue.

The dream evolved into an outdoor scene. It was a large, grassy, open field. There were now a couple hundred devotees. There was a distinctly fun and playful atmosphere. At some point, David started singing a line from a song, wanting to remind us of this particular, fun song. Much to my surprise, many people in the crowd seemed to be very familiar with this song and I realized that it must've been a show tune from a Broadway musical or a movie. It was very upbeat, and some people started singing it and doing a dance that apparently was choreographed and fitting for the song.

Then an amazing thing happened—a strong voice started to be obvious above the rest and many people started pausing and looking for where this voice was coming from. I realized that it was coming from a particular man who was among the crowd. He was tall and substantial, had an amazing, perfect, highly professional voice and was costumed ideally for the song. He was commanding such attention and obviously having so much fun and joy performing this song, which David had started with only a few words or one line. I noticed that as this was occurring

David was somewhere in the midst of the crowd. I was thinking that maybe David would pause or change the activity but somehow, he seemed perfectly happy with it and the singer became the focus of the crowd's attention.

The situation ended up being a special party, filled with fun and happy devotees who had gathered to be with David. Near the end of this wonderful performance I woke up and then I was thinking about how awesome and fun the dream was. It reminded me of David's sense of humor and that he often reminded us that God is fun, God is humor, God is playful. This dream helped me feel very connected, when my humanness had me struggling with some fear, uncertainty and concern. I am so grateful that God and David gave me this wonderful experience. There are various times, since he left the body, when I feel close to David, but this time was the first that was about fun, humor and play.

om sri ram jai ram jai jai ram om sri ram jai ram jai jai ram

WHERE'S THE FUN IN THAT?

THIS EVENT TOOK PLACE some time after David had left the body. But time and space and the "great divide" between the temporal and physical life that we live upon this planet and the life of a fully-realized soul is but child's play for the fully-realized soul.

So, I was having some challenges with one of our fellow devotees. It was upsetting me and I could see no way out of it, immersed in the middle of it emotionally as I was at the time. One day I was out walking, with my hands in my pockets, pondering the whole matter, when a thought occurred to me, and I expressed it spontaneously, addressing David inwardly. I said, "David, I wish you had taken care of this better. It would have made life easier for the rest of us."

Quick as a flash within me, a whispered voice full of humour and full of mirth responded thus: "Where's the fun in that?"

I recognized it as Davidji's voice.

om sri ram jai ram jai jai ram om sri ram jai ram jai jai ram

FAVORITE TIMES WITH DAVID: Christmas always. I always enjoyed the times I was able to go to Cloud Mountain when David was there. In particular, I remember a weekend Silent Retreat. We all went out for a walk after dinner. Between David and Larry, everyone was laughing so hard. We all tried to muffle the sounds of laughter. I can still feel the joy of that evening in my heart. Somehow, through writing, everyone was in on the jokes. And, honestly, most of the time, we were in silence, but I think Ram let us off the hook on that one.

om sri ram jai ram jai jai ram om sri ram jai ram jai jai ram

I HAVE ONE FUNNY STORY about David.

I was quite the rule follower when I was young. During a time I was at David's house, we were going to get a movie and a smoothie and he drove us there in his little green truck. He drove in the clearly marked Exit and parked in a non-parking spot! I was internally laughing because at this point I had figured out that when David did something unique it was most likely to teach me a lesson. The lesson was that I needed to lighten up.

om sri ram jai ram jai jai ram om sri ram jai ram jai jai ram

David at the confluence of the Columbia
and Snake Rivers, Washington, 2017

DAVID'S PASSING

SUDDENLY IN JULY, knowing David was unwell was an unpleasant surprise. As days passed there was a need to prepare my mind for separation. The thought came, "Oh really, will I never meet David again?" The last time he was in Ashram in 2013, it seemed David was the Divine Friend who would never, never leave us.

But when it happened on 12th August, for two days there was acceptance that David is no more amidst us. But soon after, there was a feeling that he was with me. My mind now started understanding what a friend meant when she said she did not feel her father's absence even after his passing. She and her father were like friends. Yet God chose to not give the sorrow of separation to the bereaved one.

True, we will never see our beloved David, smiling, answering questions, speaking about Satchidanand Swamiji with all love, telling us to not be complacent on the path, encouraging us to go forward, accepting everything as package from the Divine.

Yet David is here, with us in the deep silence; with us, in the friendliness we see around us...

We always saw with great joy, Pujya Swamiji looking at David and giving a very, very special smile. He would extend his hand towards David and both would sit together holding hands. Now too, they are together, both there and here.

In November, three months after David left the body, his friends from Seattle were here. They proved that David lived more strongly than ever before.

Swamiji, David, bless us all . . .

Om Sri Ram Jai Jai Jai Ram

om sri ram jai ram jai jai ram om sri ram jai ram jai jai ram

GURU BHAI, GURU BIN

IN THE LATE 90S David and I traveled to India to do a Yatra with Cate, Larry and Swami Vishwananda. David and I went first, traveling for a few weeks in the north: Haridwar, Rishikesh, Dwarahat, and then on to Agra, Meher Baba's ashram and the ashram of Sai Baba of Shirdi. Very quickly we learned that it was not acceptable for a single man and a single woman to travel together, (even if they did stay in different rooms), but thankfully a devotee from YSS informed us that, if we were Guru Bhai and Guru Bin (spiritual brother and sister), then yes, it would be "more acceptable" so we officially became spiritual brother and sister.

And now, on July 23rd, 21 years after that time in India, David was in the hospital in Everett, WA. His body was having challenge after challenge and he had cancer and pneumonia. On that day I found myself saying to John, my husband, "It is all I can do, to not go to Everett!" I knew that David needed as much space as possible to let the doctors do their jobs and that he be allowed to rest, but he was not responding to the treatments to cure him of this newest challenge: pneumonia. All this was in the forefront of my mind when two days later I could not stand the pressure of the silent command any longer: "NOW!!!! DAVID!!!, NOW!!!!" The sound and urgency of this command filled every molecule of space in my universe; there was no space left for one drop of resistance; the pull felt like a 'magnetar'.

Finally on Thursday afternoon I sent an email to Carla, doing my very best not to intrude or give any inkling that I had this loud, inner command, but saying as diplomatically as I could... "If you think Reiki might help, I would come." The answer came back from David and Carla: Yes, David has always found your Reiki to be helpful. "Great," I wrote back, "I'll be on the first ferry in the morning," and right then I began a wordless communication with David; deafeningly loud, yet silent, spirit words, sent along that cord that connected us; words that might simply be interpreted as "I'M COMING!"

I left on the first ferry on Friday, took two more ferries and drove to the hospital in Everett. When I got there Carla told me that David had been asking for me. He was sitting up in his chair and looking out the window; tears rolled down his face when he saw me, and he took my hand. I was so happy to see him; it seemed like it had been such a long time, but I couldn't wait to get my hands on his body to Reiki him, so I immediately sat down and put my hands on his feet. He began speaking to me in a whisper (because his voice had been affected by some of his medications). I stood up and moved closer to his lips so that I could hear his words. He whispered, "I was in the land of the dead and I heard your voice calling to me, so I came back!" It took a few moments for me to process what he had said (in truth I'm still processing it), and I told him how grateful I was that God had used me in that way, for "indeed we are Guru Bhai, Guru Bin."

For the next three days I visited with David, immersed in that bright and beautiful Light that is 'David', giving him Reiki, sharing stories with him (and Carla) and I stood by as the nurses monitored his vital signs. I bathed in the love that David and Carla shared with each other, in the small secret words and gestures that they had discovered in that love, and I experienced first-hand the feeling of that love and that joy as it flowed between them. It was a blessing for me.

At the end of my time there David seemed to slip back into another place, and I realized my time there was at an end. I drove back to Canada, a bit puzzled, but trusting that God's plan was perfect. Then the news came two days later that David was in hospice and the end was close at hand. What DID God have in mind?

And now, from this new vantage point, given to me by the gift of time, I see that what was given was more time. Not enough time for David to finish publishing Mother's books, which was his deepest wish, but time for me to have three special, joyful, heartfelt days with him, time for his devotees to visit with him, time for us all to meditate with him, either in the hospital or in our own homes, time for family, the ministers and time for Carla to read the emails from those who wanted to reach out with their hearts and words one last time to touch that beautiful Light we all knew as 'David'. We all had 19 more days, nineteen precious days.

I feel blessed to have been given the opportunity for God to have used my voice to call him back for that time of closure and I give thanks to a most loving God, for giving me this beautiful Spiritual Brother to play with in this lifetime.

om sri ram jai ram jai jai ram om sri ram jai ram jai jai ram

HIS PASSING FROM the physical form was devastating. I could not understand why God would physically take David from us. But then realizing he hasn't left me, he is just a different form. Now I need to listen and do a reset as David and the Masters have shown us. That is the point, I suppose, to be able to reset or be in spiritual bliss at all times.

David's compassion was always evident and he gave me what was needed to grow in God and I must keep this uppermost in my life.

om sri ram jai ram jai jai ram om sri ram jai ram jai jai ram

EVER SINCE BELOVED Davidji left the body in Mahasamadhi, I've been grieving. Every day, tears have fallen. My heart has ached inconsolably as cherished memories have flooded my thoughts, each one flavored with that Unconditional Love only a true Master can shower upon his or her devotee.

Of course I've known—intellectually, that is— that my most beloved Teacher is now free of all physical pain, that he is released from that "heavy lead overcoat," the body, and that now his radiance shines ever more brightly and his power to help all suffering humanity is now unlimited. But each time I'd surrender this grief, laying it all at my Lord's feet, soon afterwards I'd take it right back again, even admitting that at times what I'd felt had shades of a "pity-me-party" to it.

Then, only a few days ago in fact, Divine Grace created an opening within me, and with it, fertile ground in which to plant the seed of awareness that this grief has been blocking God's joy-filled Presence from entering in.

Mother once told the story of the soul who, upon entering the Pearly Gates, couldn't help but notice an enormous room filled with packages, all addressed to people on earth. Upon enquiring, this soul found out that these gifts could not be delivered. Why? Because the people had kept all of their doors and windows closed. They were not yet open to receiving all that God had in store for them.

Now, through Grace alone, I am choosing to keep my doors and windows open. Through Grace alone, I will remember to identify myself with the Projectionist in the booth, rather than that which He is playfully projecting onto the screen of duality. Aum Sri Ram Jai Ram. Victory to God in all the Masters!

om sri ram jai ram jai jai ram om sri ram jai ram jai jai ram

DAVID WAS WONDERFUL in his correspondence. Once when I was feeling grief, he wrote me this passage, which I forwarded to Carla shortly after David left the body, and she responded "This is a message from God." David wrote:

"This world will always present us with reasons for feelings of loss, but the good news is there is a solution. When we surrender all to the Infinite Beloved, giving God our joys and sorrows, giving Him our all and laying it at His feet, and really letting it go, then He takes our burden and lifts it from us.

When we empty ourselves of our sorrows, our loneliness, all that weighs us down, then He may fill that emptied cup with His bliss, peace and joy. Never forget, dear One, that you are made in His likeness and image. In your essence, you are a being of Light.

When you look out through these two eyes and see only darkness, it is only a veil that has been drawn down around you. Look deeper, and you will see His Light shining in and around you. I have gone through darkness, through sorrow and feeling alone, I have felt the grief of the world, and I know that God ever stands at the ready to lift us up, if we will let Him.

It is natural to feel such grief at times, but be sure not to nurture it, but give it to God. Do not be identified with it, but see it passing through you, breathing it through, letting it go. When you do this, it will pass, and God will come in and comfort you—this, I know. Be at peace, dear one."

om sri ram jai ram jai jai ram om sri ram jai ram jai jai ram

I AM SO GRATEFUL that I embraced every moment that I could to see him in person and to benefit from his powerful spiritual energy.

I saw him with a group of devotees shortly before he died. He could hardly talk; he leaned over and whispered something to his wife Carla. Carla said, "David wants you all to keep God on your mind."

om sri ram jai ram jai jai ram om sri ram jai ram jai jai ram

A God-Man Among Us

DAVID ANSWERS AN UNSPOKEN PRAYER

SOMEWHERE BACK THERE in time, as I was chanting Ram Nam, I experienced doubt that I was chanting Ramdas's version of Ram Nam accurately. This was starting to weigh on my mind and I thought I'd need to ask David for clarification when he next visited our Centre.

A month or two later, David came to town and on Sunday morning I showed up early and I took my place in a chair in the front row, just to the right of where David would be sitting. I closed my eyes, settled myself down and started meditating.

David came into the room and took his place on the chair at the front of the room. He closed his eyes and meditated for a few minutes. He then quite noticeably shifted his chair to the left so that it was now facing partly in my direction.

He started service by saying that he was going to teach us to chant Ram Nam "the way that

Ramdas taught it to Mother". And he proceeded to do so.

All of this took place without David and myself communicating verbally on the subject of chanting Ramdas's Ram Nam accurately.

om sri ram jai ram jai jai ram om sri ram jai ram jai jai ram

JUST BEING NEAR our beloved teacher, David, was truly an honour and a sacred privilege!

I renewed my contact with David at his and Carla's Mt Vernon house about 20 years after my Guru, Mother Hamilton, left the body.

I seldom, if ever, had questions for Mother or David—I preferred to bask in their God glow. However, on this occasion I had wanted three wishes granted that only God and I knew about. During our precious time together that day, David granted all three wishes with a twinkle in his eye and with very little fanfare!

This was the start of my relationship with a fully realized master, and dear friend, David.

om sri ram jai ram jai jai ram om sri ram jai ram jai jai ram

OBSERVING A GOD-MAN

THE EAGLE:

THE FIRST TIME I saw an animal's reaction to David was at Yellowstone National Park in October 2016. We had arrived at the nearby campground that afternoon and wanted to take a short drive into the park before it got dark. The first place that we stopped was along a medium sized river right beside the road, where several cars had pulled over at the small parking lot. Everyone was looking at a bald eagle perched very high up on a dead sort of tree on the opposite side of the river.

David took his camera and stood where he was exactly opposite the eagle. The whole time we were there, the eagle was facing to the side; all the other "photographers" were snapping the side view of the eagle as he never moved his head. David was standing there about a minute and the eagle turned his regal head and stared directly at David. He looked at him for only a few seconds, long enough for David to take the picture and then the eagle turned away. I know that the eagle sensed that David wanted his photo, so he turned at the exact right moment for David to get the shot. It was quite something to watch.

THE CRANE:

WE WERE RIDING our bikes in San Antonio, Texas around mid-March 2017 on our pilgrimage across the USA. I had seen this very tall and stately crane in the water next to the bike path and pointed him out to David. He stopped, turned around and got out his camera. He stood about 20 feet away and had his camera, taking pictures.

The crane was looking sideways and then after only a couple of minutes, the bird starting walking in a circle and then doubled back and started coming towards David. He got in the perfect position for David to take the photo, looking right at David at times and then other times posing for him too, so that he was able to get a perfect shot of this elegant and graceful bird. Again, I was just amazed to see how the animal was quietly but most determinedly posing for David and his camera.

THE COW:

THIS IS THE ONE that is truly INCREDIBLE. We were walking around the HUGE building where they had the Texas rodeo, fair, and animal show. We were in Houston visiting my college roommate and were waiting for the rodeo to start. Most of the cows were all gone as it was the last day of the animal exhibitions that had been going on for three weeks.

There was a small shed that had the animals that were "best in show," which included cows, sheep, goats, etc. There were two cows in a pen and they had signs above each showing their worth at $350,000 each! One of the cows had its back to us and the other was facing us, both laying down. I walked in and saw them and then walked out. I pointed them out to David and he started walking into this shed. I stood outside the shed, watching through a window.

As soon as David walked in this little shed, the cow facing us stood up and looked at David. She kept her eyes only on David; there were many people all around and that cow just looked right at David. It was remarkable. As soon as David walked into that shed, that cow stood up and stared at him. She knew who David was and was acknowledging his greatness. It was incredible. Even at this moment, I can still feel and see how David and this magnificent creature were bound together in a Sea of Light. A connection that made time stand still.

It is a great honor and blessing to be able to observe a God-man, and a powerful reminder of how God operates in every moment in such delightful and surprising ways!

om sri ram jai ram jai jai ram om sri ram jai ram jai jai ram

I WAS ANXIOUS, preparing to go into surgery for breast cancer, this very morning.

Suddenly in the larch tree, right outside my window, an enormous Barn Owl appeared! It looked straight at me for several minutes, as if solving a puzzle—then flew away.

I emailed David to ask him whether this was a "good omen"? David wrote back almost immediately: "All of Nature responds to a soul seeking communion with God."

When I entered the hospital, the nurse said, "There was an Enormous Owl perched right outside the entrance, 'as if conducting his business'".

I knew then that God was offering complete protection, whatever the outcome.

It did not mean it would be painless.

I heard Sri Yuktewar say: "REMAIN DIS-PASSIONATE."

I realised later how many surgeries David would undergo with his "saintly surgeons".

om sri ram jai ram jai jai ram om sri ram jai ram jai jai ram

ONCE I WAS AT DAVID's house and had been going through a time of wondering if God was even real. I had a secret wish that I had told no one. Very secret. I wanted to be like the person in *Autobiography of a Yogi* who had a talisman appear in her hand. As we were meditating, I heard David get up and walk behind my chair. He said put out your hand. So I did. Then he put a polished rock in my hand. I had my talisman.

After, David told me that was one of the strangest requests God had made of him because he had no clue why God would want to give me a rock but he did it because he knew there had to be a reason. That explanation to me was even more of a lesson than the talisman. Following God's direction even when you don't understand or can't see a possible reason. Trust the direction.

David was / is a great influence in my life. He is still guiding and there in Spirit. But sometimes I just want to go to his house and have a cup of tea and sit with him in his physical form.

om sri ram jai ram jai jai ram om sri ram jai ram jai jai ram

GOD'S OMNISCIENCE THROUGH DAVID

THROUGH DAVID I LEARNED that a God-realized soul, whose individual consciousness has found its true home in oneness with all, shares a deep, intimate connection to each and every part of God. United with the all-pervading source, access to all knowledge becomes available to that one. The relationship God so lovingly weaves between

Guru and disciple is the most thrilling and precious experience of this omniscient spirit of oneness. God blessed me with the following example
of his all-knowing, omnipresent love through
David.

One summer, a fellow devotee and I had the
opportunity to travel to Master's holy sites in
California. In preparation for the trip, we asked
David for his blessings on the pilgrimage, which
he readily gave. He said that as a young disciple
in the 1970s, he himself had gone on a Yogananda
pilgrimage and visited Lake Shrine, Mount
Washington and the Encinitas Hermitage, and
had felt the spiritual power and connection to
Master at those places. Both of us devotees had
older cars, and in David's loving-kindness and
practical wisdom, he actually loaned us his and
Carla's own car so we would have something comfortable and reliable for our long pilgrimage drive.
We were humbled to dust by his care and concern.
We felt David's blessing, protection, guidance and
presence with us everywhere we went on that
trip, and absolutely every moment at every turn
was pure Grace of God and Guru.

Upon returning, David kindly invited me to
come to his home to talk about the trip—what we
saw and did and how it all went. David listened

patiently, and after sharing with him many wonderful highlights, I had one significant experience yet to tell him, which was a singularly unforgettable revelation in my soul's connection to the Gurus of this path. I began by saying, "Something happened to me at this certain place. It was so powerful. Shall I tell you about it?" David paused and looked at me softly and directly. The smile that lit his face was gentle and warm, yet his reply hit me with such astonishing force, it was like a hurricane smashed through my whole being and I just about fell off my chair. I am quite sure the earth shifted on its axis at that moment. At least, the earth of the limited sphere of my consciousness was definitely shifted. With his knowing smile, he said, "If you like. It would be nice to hear it in your own words."

I did not need to tell David what had happened because my Guru had been there with me in that experience—in every experience! By the power of God in his simple reply, the realization hit me that He is seeing through my eyes, breathing through my breath, thinking through my thoughts, feeling through my heart—He is in me and I am in Him, He is my own Self, and I am a part of His own Being. David was a perfect open doorway to God, and in the moment he spoke those words, it felt as if I had been swept through the door of my Guru into a glimpse of the omniscient omnipresence of God Absolute. Jai Guru.

om sri ram jai ram jai jai ram om sri ram jai ram jai jai ram

A GIFT FROM DAVID

THE LAST EMAIL that I sent to David before he left the body was challenging for me, so I asked Mother for help. From that point on, the writing of the note for David went better. First, I settled myself within my Self, observed my inner state and then wrote my note. I reported to David that I was, "experiencing the Joy of living this life". Which is as it was.

That sense of Joy stayed with me steadily for the most part, lasting several days past his leaving the body, and it even intensified noticeably after he had left his body. I felt a little bit guilty about that, considering that David's leave-taking from his body would probably not have been pleasant, looking at it from the human perspective.

About two or three days after David had left the body, I drove down to the mall near where I live. I parked in my favorite area of the parking lot and got out of my car, intending to walk over to the Starbucks outlet and have a cup of coffee.

As an aside, I am of the view that there are times that come upon us in this life when a good cup of coffee and perhaps a piece of chocolate is all that we can manage effectively.

It seems that I ought to add here that it was not as if I was actually grieving at the time. I knew I'd be missing David but as for grief...no, not really. As mentioned earlier I was experiencing this wave of Joy pouring through me. And I had somehow concluded that David's life and even his leaving the body was a great triumph, a great victory. And that was how I had explained David's leaving the body to one of my spiritual friends at work.

Plus, it had occurred to me that without David among us in the body, my life, that is to say, this Spiritual Life, was clearly and irrevocably now in my own hands so to speak. It was now very much up to me. So, you could perhaps say that mentally, I was "girding my loins", getting myself ready for the road ahead rather than grieving.

"*Wherefore gird up the loins of your mind, be sober, and hope to the end for the grace that is to be brought unto you at the revelation of Jesus Christ;*" (1 Peter 1:13)

As I was walking toward the mall entrance, and I'm not quite sure how else to explain this, but David came fully into my conscious awareness as an actual Presence. You might say that he sort of took me over at some level for a little stretch of time. (Not quite fully a clear explanation but it's the best I can do for now.)

David then gave me two experiences, each of which lasted several minutes. First, he showed me what a Saint might experience. So that was a full sense of God "with me, within me and everywhere around me", to borrow a phrase from Ramdas. But at the same time there was a small separation where I could step back and see this drama unfolding in my life from a small distance. And I could move my consciousness back and forth between those two states of awareness. You might say that I was in the middle of the experience and then also observing it unfolding from a small distance.

Next, David showed me what a Fully-Realized soul might experience. This is more difficult to describe and I can really only approximate it as I do not have sufficient words to describe it better at this time. But the main thing was that there was no separation. Everything was God. Everything was God Experience.

I must add that it wasn't as if I was out-of-body! I was very much solidly in the body and strolling comfortably and pleasantly toward the coffee shop, although here and there during this experience I found myself pause in order to focus more fully; experience more fully; enjoy more fully.

But throughout that part of the experience there was no division. No separate sense of God and me and David, or the mall parking lot for that matter. It was all seamlessness. I felt very much at ease and comfortable in God, as all and all-in-all. Again, borrowing a phrase from the Masters.

I continued on, strolling toward the coffee shop. And probably smiling quite inexplicably to anyone observing on the outside.

My experiences with Mother and Master and David in this life make it clear to me that these Great Masters can reach out and touch us with their Grace and their Blessings effortlessly. And that they are very much involved in our welfare, and in our spiritual development. Supporting us, guiding us, probably often without our even realizing it.

om sri ram jai ram jai jai ram om sri ram jai ram jai jai ram

I WAS GIVEN THE GIFT from God to know what He was doing through David. It is something God has seen fit for me to know and it is quite wonderful. I feel deep gratitude for God's love, in trying to help us get back to Him, through beloved David as His instrument.

om sri ram jai ram jai jai ram om sri ram jai ram jai jai ram

THIS IS AN EXCERPT from an email that I sent to David on August 2, 1999. In it I tell him how his presence was influencing me and how these experiences aided me in appraising his spiritual state.

Dear David,

For the last couple of weeks, it has been on my mind to tell you how much I appreciate all that you have done for God, for Mother, and for me. I finally decided to write you in this way. In the first couple of months after Mother's passing, I twice had the interesting experience before service at your home of strongly feeling Mother's presence entering the room. At both these times, the feeling coincided just before your entry into the room. I remember looking up at you in surprise because the sense of Mother was so strong. I took this as confirmation from Mother that you had received her mantle and had her complete support. Though I knew this mentally before, the inner experience of feeling Mother come in this way through you was accompanied by the knowledge that she was using this method of confirming it inwardly for me.

In late 1994 and in 1995 I had another type of experience several times in your presence. Though I only told you about it one time—once while it was happening because it was so evident in me and I wanted to explain myself—it actually happened four or five times. Each time it happened the sequence of events was the same. It started by hearing your voice in normal conversation. A spiritual current seemed to emanate from your voice itself. I experienced being wrapped in a cocoon of silence, my consciousness withdrawing from my body senses and being filled with a deep bliss. God showed me the spiritual power that was coming from your voice. I took this as confirmation that you had succeeded in going through the second crucifixion, that of the throat center. From this point on your writing and speaking ability in the Spirit was markedly more profound and seemed more spontaneous than ever. Also, after this, devotees started being directed to you by God. A short while later, I found in Meher Baba's writings a statement confirming that after going through the fifth chakra, a person is a fit instrument to be a guru.

In the summer of 1995, once while we were talking about Mother, I was lifted up into a rapture and you may remember tears pouring from my eyes and my withdrawing from the body. After this, this experience happened many times while in your presence, though with less outward display. Also in later episodes, I sometimes witnessed the effulgence of God sparkling and twirling about you. The very air was filled with a gossamer fog-like substance made up of dancing bubbles of light and twinkling stars. I sometimes heard the OM roar of many waters. I know this sounds like fairyland, but I mention these details simply to be as accurate and as complete as I can.

A couple of weeks ago, you came into the room for Wednesday night service and sat next to me while we listened to one of Mother's talks. As you sat down, there was a twinkle in your eye. Inwardly, God told me that I would like what would happen as a result of sitting next to you in whatever state you were in at the time. God told me to pay attention and I did. The subtle divine current that emanated from you so lifted me up that I experienced unfathomable ecstasy for many hours after. That night, I felt as though I was awake while my body slept. I was feeling a continuous divine current that was set up in me through contact with you. Every nerve in my body pulsed with bliss, my heart fluttered and so did my eyes. This lasted for several days in lessening degrees. Thank you for that experience. I feel that it is just a small part of the bliss that you have been experiencing.

Though I am not able to confirm the state of your being, whether you have "gone over the top" or not, I feel that whatever it is that God has brought you to is worthy of note, that your spiritual attainment is a rare thing on this Earth. I thank God and Mother and Master for this wonderful blessing that is your life among us.

om sri ram jai ram jai jai ram om sri ram jai ram jai jai ram

FOR DAVID: MY GURU

MY GURU is made of Truth.

Not simply that He speaks the truth or that He lives in truth.

The very atoms collected into the form of my Guru are composed of nothing but the One Absolute, Vital, Living Truth.

My Guru is made of Love.

The attracting force of pure Love alone binds the molecules of my Guru's body together.

Were this Love to release - poof! No more body! He is merged into All-space.

My Guru is made of Humility.

At all times He is ablaze with the power, heat and light of a thousand suns.

But He keeps it secret, in His golden cloak, so as not to burn me up too quick!

My Guru is made of Patience.

With such tender patience He holds my hand, walking every step with me, slowly,

because my legs are very short and His are very long.

My Guru is made of Good Cheer.

Though He bears the weight of worlds, He is ever-light, ever-free, ever-fun, ever full, dancing in the Joy of Life.

My Guru is made of Wisdom.

Having gone beyond all knowledge into the Ocean of Omniscience, He returned to teach all sincere hearts who might hear.

My Guru is made of God.

Thank God for my Guru!

David at Union Creek, Oregon, 2010

"It is with a full heart that I know I will miss seeing you in body, but I am comforted by the fact that we are ever one in Spirit. Just as in other transitions in the past—such as when I left my occupation in order to serve you fulltime; the pilgrimages He has taken me to in sacred India; my year in silence and solitude—these have all benefited more than myself and I know that this pilgrimage will do so as well. So with full confidence I set out on this journey knowing that through His power we will all continue to grow together in Divine Consciousness. My continued love and blessings to you."

DAVID, SEPTEMBER 18, 2015

APPENDIX

FROM SWAMI MUKTANANDA, Anandashram, Kerala, India, on David's passing:

> ... What wells up in our mind at this point are the fond memories of the long association of Davidji and all of you with the Ashram from the late 1990s, and how he was highly influenced by the inspiring life and mission of Beloved Papa, Param Pujya Mataji and more deeply connected with Param Pujya Swami Satchidanandaji. Davidji's radiant face with the ever smiling, loving and blissful approach endeared himself to everyone at the Ashram.

> Though Davidji fell sick very seriously and was hospitalised many a times, what is more striking is the stoic self he possessed in spite of the untold stress at the physical level. The dedicated, loving, patient service rendered by you in taking care of Davidji and also updating all friends about his state of health periodically is really remarkable and touching.

Vinobaji's words on Gandhiji's passing away seems relevant to be quoted here:
"When I heard of Bapuji's death my imme-
diate reaction was: now he has become
immortal. Time has only strengthened that
conviction. When Bapu was in the body,
it took time to go and meet him; now it
takes no time at all. All I need do is close
my eyes and I am with him. When he was
alive I buried myself in his work, and went
to talk with him only now and then. Now,
I talk with him all the time and feel his
presence near me. The sages speak to us of
the immense range of the soul, the Self; we
reverently accept their teaching. So long as
a great soul lives in the body his power is
limited, but when he is released from the
body his power knows no bounds."

We also remember how keen he was, to
be in Ashram in November 2019 to take
part in the concluding programme of Pujya
Swamiji's birth centenary year. Though not
in physical body anymore, he will continue
to be a source of great inspiration and guidance to innumerable spiritual aspirants.
Deepest love to you all,
Muktananda

WRITTEN AND READ by Carla Hickenbottom at the funeral service for Yogacharya David:

LOVE, that is what David was and is all about.

When I first met him, I knew right away that there was something very special about him. As my Guru, closest friend and husband, I have been privileged and blessed beyond any words that can describe to have been able to be with him for the last 25 years. He spent all the time we were together focused on bringing myself and all of you back to God, to knowing our Oneness with our Heavenly Father.

What was it like living with my Guru? I was asked that by Corliss at Anandashram and I answered "Unfathomable." I knew that I was only experiencing a very small part of who David really is. He saved my life and all the years before meeting him was really preparation for my becoming his devotee but also his friend and life partner. All these years we were together and very rarely apart.

Of course, different things came up but we really never argued. It was more about talking through what "worked and didn't work" in our relationship and sorting through the intricacies of living in the world. The only times he really got angry and let me know about it was when I wasn't doing my work, that I was afraid to talk to him out of fear or shame. He would say, I don't care how bad it is, as long as you talk to me about it, it will be okay. In the marriage vows, we really stressed to each other the importance of "forgiveness" and he taught me that time and time again through his example of loving kindness.

He used to say that the thing that made him the happiest was when the devotees did their own work. He was fun, generous, kind, sweet, gentle, clear and had such a warm and engaging sense of humor. He would often say, "What's the fun!" He always loved how God presented new adventures for us and he would say that God would do that in the most "unexpected and delightful" ways.

While serving David in the body I was focused on his physical form and needs, and I knew and often experienced who he was in God. I now feel and experience the absolute true nature of all of his love, both human and divine.

I want to now tell you about what I witnessed and heard him say the last few days he was here. Up until the very end, he was still very present and when I would talk to him, especially the last few days, he didn't respond to me but then all of a sudden, I would say something and he would either whisper something or nod his head.

Seeing him lying there in the bed, I asked him, "What is the purpose of all this?" And he said, "To focus on God." He said: "God is beyond the light." "God touched me on the forehead." "JOY, JOY . . . why not?"

For about two days he had his eyes like Lahiri Mahasaya with the left eye half open and the right eye closed. He said he saw his circle of love expanding out from the room, the community, country and to all this world.

The day he left, God directed me to wash him in the holy Ganges water that had been brought previously by Jill. I took a white cotton washcloth and bathed him in this sacred water and chanted "God, Christ, Gurus" while doing so and the experience was so very blissful and extremely powerful.

On August 12, all afternoon and early evening, I felt that I couldn't stay in the room; it wasn't that I was being pushed out, or that he didn't want me there, it was more that it was just "too full" and Ruth helped me realize he was expanding more and more and into the Light of God.

I would like to end with what he had written to me for my birthday in 2014. Reverend Jill had made me a cardboard, fabric covered cake and on the large bottom layer, she had fellow devotees write short messages for my birthday which were so loving and thoughtful. On the top layer, in the smaller box were messages from David and I wanted to share these with all of you as I know that it is a gift for all of us.

- Surrender to God brings peace.
- The surest sign of union with God is ever-new Joy.
- Union with God is a deep connection with all humanity.
- LOVE—is the one eternal constant.
- Seva is love made visible.
- God and Guru's blessings are ever with you.
- In service—one to another—we are lifted higher and higher.

FOR MORE INFORMATION about Yogacharya David, Mother Hamilton, and their path, visit www.crossandlotus.com. David's and Mother's talks are available here, as well as The Cross and The Lotus Journal, David's blog, spiritual music, information about this Guru-lineage, and much more. These are all available free of charge.

The Cross and The Lotus Publishing is dedicated to publishing the writings and teachings of our gurus, Reverend Yogacharya Mother Hamilton (1904–1991) and Reverend Yogacharya David Hickenbottom (1954–2019). We are dedicated to realizing God and serving devotees of every race, color, creed and religion. We bow at the feet of the masters in our Guru-lineage, and to saints and realized masters of all religions.

ABOUT THE MANTRA Om Sri Ram Jai Ram Jai Jai Ram

This mantra, also referred to as "Ram Nam," is translated as "Victory to God." Om stands for the cosmic creative Word of God. Sri denotes great reverence. Ram is a name of God. Jai means "glory to" or "victory to." The use of God's name in this way is aimed to lift the consciousness of spiritual aspirants, and acts as a protection and a blessing. Swami Ramdas said, "When we tune ourselves with the Name, we tune ourselves with God."

Mother Hamilton and Yogacharya David practiced the repetition of this mantra which was taught to Mother by Swami Ramdas. They, in turn, taught aspirants to repeat Ram Nam with love at all times, mentally or aloud, as a simple and effective means of connecting with the presence of God.

Acknowledgements

My DEEPEST APPRECIATION to all those who took time and made the effort to put pen to paper (or fingers to keyboard) and contribute to this book. Without you, there would be no book. Every reader shares this gratitude, as your experiences become theirs.

Warmest thanks to Carla Hickenbottom for spearheading this volume, to Rebecca Harvey, Judy Ellis and Cate Koler for hours of proofreading, advice, and continuing encouragement, and to Michael Victory for polishing and formatting the included photos. A special nod to Jan Westendorp of Kato Design and Photo for applying her professional skills and energy to this volume.

And our immeasurable gratitude to Davidji for sharing this incarnation with us. We are truly blessed.

www.ingramcontent.com/pod-product-compliance
Lightning Source LLC
Chambersburg PA
CBHW071400120626
46546CB00002B/761